Business Innovation Unleashed

Strategies for Staying Ahead in a Competitive Market

PEARL HILL

The presentation of the information is without contract or any type of guarantee assurance. The trademarks that are used are without any consent, and the publication of the trademark is without permission or backing by the trademark owner. All trademarks and brands within this book are for clarifying purposes only and are the owned by the owners themselves, not affiliated with this document.

Table of Contents

Chapter 1

Introduction

The Importance of Innovation in Business

Innovation plays a pivotal role in the success and longevity of any business. It is the driving force behind differentiation, growth, and competitive advantage. Without innovation, businesses become stagnant, unable to adapt to the ever-changing market dynamics. The essence of innovation lies in the ability to foresee trends, meet evolving customer needs, and enhance operational efficiencies.

In the early stages of business development, innovation often manifests in the form of unique products or services. Entrepreneurs tap into unaddressed market gaps, offering novel solutions. For instance, the inception of ride-sharing services revolutionized urban transportation, addressing the inefficiencies and limitations of traditional taxi services. This kind of product innovation is crucial for startups looking to carve out a niche in competitive landscapes.

However, innovation is not confined to products alone. Process innovation is equally significant. By rethinking and optimizing internal processes, businesses can achieve remarkable improvements in productivity and cost-efficiency. A classic example is the implementation of lean manufacturing principles in the automotive industry. By minimizing waste and streamlining production workflows, companies like Toyota have set new benchmarks in efficiency and quality.

Customer-centric innovation is another vital aspect. Understanding and anticipating customer needs can lead to the development of groundbreaking products and services. This requires businesses to cultivate a deep understanding of their target audience through market research, customer feedback, and data analytics. Consider the tech giant Apple, which consistently innovates by focusing on user experience. Its ecosystem of products and services is designed to seamlessly integrate, providing unparalleled convenience and satisfaction to its customers.

Innovation also plays a crucial role in business model transformation. Disruptive innovations often give rise to entirely new business models that can redefine industries. The subscription-based model, popularized by companies like Netflix and Spotify, has transformed the entertainment industry. By offering unlimited access to content for a monthly fee, these companies have not only created a sustainable revenue stream but also significantly altered consumer behavior and expectations.

Fostering a culture of innovation within an organization is essential. This involves creating an environment where creativity and experimentation are encouraged, and failure is seen as a stepping stone to success. Leadership plays a critical role in this regard. Leaders must inspire and motivate their teams to think outside the box, take calculated risks, and embrace change. Google's 20% time policy, which allows employees to dedicate a portion of their workweek to pursue innovative projects, is a testament to how fostering creativity can lead to groundbreaking ideas.

Collaboration is another key factor in driving innovation. Cross-functional teams, diverse in their expertise and perspectives, can generate more creative solutions than individuals working in silos. Open innovation, which involves collaborating with external partners such as universities, research institutions, and other companies, can also amplify a business's innovative capabilities. By leveraging external knowledge and resources, businesses can accelerate their innovation processes and bring new products and services to market more swiftly.

The role of technology in innovation cannot be overstated. Technological advancements provide businesses with new tools and platforms to innovate. Artificial intelligence, big data, and the Internet of Things are transforming industries by enabling businesses to analyze vast amounts of data, automate processes, and create connected ecosystems. For instance, predictive analytics can help retailers optimize inventory management by predicting demand patterns, while IoT-enabled devices can provide real-time data to improve operational efficiency in manufacturing.

Sustainability is emerging as a significant driver of innovation. With growing awareness of environmental issues and increasing regulatory pressures, businesses are innovating to develop sustainable products and practices. This not only helps in reducing their environmental footprint but also appeals to the growing segment of environmentally conscious consumers. Companies like Tesla are at the forefront of this movement, pioneering electric vehicles and renewable energy solutions that are paving the way for a more sustainable future.

The impact of innovation on competitiveness is profound. In today's fast-paced business environment, companies that fail to innovate risk being outpaced by more agile and forward-thinking competitors. Continuous innovation enables businesses to stay ahead of the curve, anticipate market changes, and adapt accordingly. It also helps in building a strong brand reputation, as companies known for their innovative capabilities are often perceived as leaders in their respective industries.

Moreover, innovation can drive growth by opening up new markets and revenue streams. Diversification into new product lines, expansion into new geographical markets, or the introduction of new services can provide businesses with additional sources of income. This not only helps in mitigating risks associated with reliance on a single product or market but also enhances overall business resilience.

To effectively manage innovation, businesses need to adopt a strategic approach. This involves setting clear innovation goals, allocating resources, and establishing metrics to measure progress. Innovation management frameworks such as the Stage-Gate process can provide a structured approach to managing the various stages of innovation, from ideation to commercialization. This helps in ensuring that innovative ideas are systematically evaluated, developed, and brought to market.

However, managing innovation also requires flexibility and adaptability. The innovation landscape is inherently uncertain, and not all ideas will succeed. Businesses must be prepared to pivot, iterate, and refine their innovations based on feedback and changing market conditions. This iterative approach, commonly seen in agile methodologies, allows businesses to rapidly prototype, test, and improve their innovations, thereby increasing the likelihood of success.

Employee engagement is another critical component of successful innovation. Empowering employees at all levels to contribute ideas and participate in the innovation process can lead to a more dynamic and innovative organization. Techniques such as hackathons, innovation contests, and suggestion schemes can provide platforms for employees to showcase their creativity and problem-solving skills.

Finally, businesses must be mindful of the potential challenges and barriers to innovation. Resistance to change, lack of resources, and organizational inertia can impede innovation efforts. Addressing these challenges requires strong leadership, effective communication, and a commitment to fostering a culture that embraces innovation.

In conclusion, the importance of innovation in business cannot be overstated. It is the lifeblood that fuels growth, competitiveness, and long-term success. By adopting a holistic approach that encompasses product, process, customer-centric, and business model innovation, businesses can navigate the complexities of the modern market landscape and emerge as leaders in their industries. Fostering a culture of innovation, leveraging technology, and embracing sustainability are essential strategies for businesses looking to thrive in an increasingly dynamic and competitive world. To sustain innovation, businesses must continuously invest in research and development (R&D). R&D is the backbone of technological breakthroughs and product advancements. Companies like Samsung and IBM allocate significant portions of their revenue to R&D, ensuring they remain at the forefront of their industries. This investment not only drives innovation but also attracts top talent, creating a virtuous cycle of growth and advancement.

Overview of Competitive Markets

Competitive markets are dynamic environments where numerous businesses vie for the attention and loyalty of consumers. Understanding the nuanced mechanisms of these markets is crucial for any business aiming to thrive rather than merely survive. At the heart of competitive markets are several key elements: supply and demand dynamics, market structures, competitive strategies, and consumer behavior. Each of these components plays a vital role in shaping the competitive landscape and determining the success or failure of businesses within it.

The law of supply and demand is fundamental to competitive markets. It dictates that the price of goods and services is determined by the availability of those goods (supply) and the desire for them (demand). When demand exceeds supply, prices tend to rise, incentivizing producers to increase production.

Conversely, when supply exceeds demand, prices typically fall, encouraging consumers to purchase more. This delicate balance ensures that resources are allocated efficiently, and markets remain responsive to changes in consumer preferences and production capabilities.

Market structures define the competitive environment in which businesses operate. These structures range from perfect competition to monopolies, with several variations in between. In a perfectly competitive market, numerous small firms produce identical products, and no single firm has significant market power. This scenario fosters a high level of competition, driving innovation and efficiency. However, perfect competition is more theoretical than practical, as real-world markets often exhibit characteristics of oligopolies, monopolistic competition, or monopolies.

Oligopolies, for instance, are markets dominated by a few large firms that have significant control over prices and supply. The automotive and airline industries are classic examples of oligopolistic markets. These firms often engage in strategic behavior, such as price fixing or collusion, to maintain their market positions. Monopolistic competition, on the other hand, features many firms offering differentiated products. This differentiation can be based on quality, branding, or other attributes, allowing firms to gain a competitive edge. The fast-food industry is a prime example, where numerous brands compete based on taste, price, and marketing.

Monopolies exist when a single firm controls the entire market for a particular good or service, facing no competition. While monopolies can lead to higher prices and reduced consumer choice, they also result in significant economies of scale and substantial investments in research and development. Utilities and public transportation services are often natural monopolies, where high infrastructure costs make competition impractical.

Competitive strategies are crucial for businesses operating in competitive markets. These strategies can be broadly categorized into cost leadership, differentiation, and focus strategies. Cost leadership involves becoming the lowest-cost producer in the industry, allowing a business to offer lower prices than competitors. This strategy is particularly effective in price-sensitive markets where consumers prioritize cost over other factors. Walmart's success is largely attributed to its cost leadership strategy, offering a wide range of products at consistently low prices.

Differentiation, on the other hand, focuses on offering unique products or services that stand out from competitors. This can involve superior quality, innovative features, exceptional customer service, or strong brand identity. Apple's differentiation strategy, for example, has positioned it as a premium brand known for its innovative technology and sleek design. By creating products that resonate with consumers on multiple levels, businesses can command higher prices and build strong customer loyalty.

Focus strategies involve targeting a specific market segment or niche with tailored products and services. This approach allows businesses to serve the unique needs of a particular group, often with greater precision and expertise than competitors. A company like Rolex, for instance, focuses on the luxury watch market, catering to consumers who value craftsmanship, exclusivity, and prestige. By concentrating on a narrow market segment, businesses can achieve a competitive advantage and establish a strong market presence.

Understanding consumer behavior is essential for succeeding in competitive markets. Consumer preferences, purchasing habits, and decision-making processes influence the demand for products and services. Market research and data analytics provide valuable insights into these behaviors, enabling businesses to tailor their offerings and marketing strategies accordingly. For example, the rise of e-commerce has transformed consumer behavior, with convenience and accessibility becoming key drivers of purchasing decisions. Companies like Amazon have capitalized on this trend by offering a seamless online shopping experience, fast delivery, and personalized recommendations.

Brand loyalty and customer retention are critical in competitive markets. Building and maintaining a loyal customer base can provide a significant competitive advantage, as repeat customers are often more profitable than new ones. Businesses can foster loyalty through consistent quality, excellent customer service, and engaging marketing campaigns. Loyalty programs, personalized communication, and exclusive offers can also enhance customer retention. Starbucks' rewards program, for example, incentivizes repeat purchases by offering free drinks and other perks to loyal customers.

Innovation is another vital factor in maintaining competitiveness. Continuous improvement and the development of new products and services enable businesses to stay ahead of market trends and meet evolving consumer needs. Innovation can take many forms, from technological advancements to process improvements and new business models. Companies like Tesla have disrupted traditional industries through innovative electric vehicles and energy solutions, setting new standards and challenging established competitors.

Globalization has expanded the scope of competitive markets, allowing businesses to operate on an international scale. This globalization presents both opportunities and challenges. On one hand, it opens up new markets and customer bases, enabling businesses to grow and diversify. On the other hand, it increases competition, as companies must now contend with international rivals and navigate complex regulatory environments. Successful global businesses adapt their strategies to local markets while leveraging their global strengths. McDonald's, for example, tailors its menu to local tastes while maintaining its core brand identity and operational efficiencies.

Regulation and government policies also influence competitive markets. Antitrust laws, trade policies, and industry regulations can impact the level of competition and market dynamics. Governments often intervene to prevent monopolies, promote fair competition, and protect consumer interests. Understanding and complying with these regulations is crucial for businesses to operate successfully and avoid legal pitfalls.

Technological advancements continue to reshape competitive markets. Digital transformation, automation, and the rise of the internet have created new opportunities and challenges for businesses. Online platforms and digital marketing have leveled the playing field, allowing small businesses to compete with larger firms. Meanwhile, automation and advanced manufacturing technologies have increased efficiency and reduced costs, enabling businesses to compete on a global scale.

In conclusion, competitive markets are complex and multifaceted, requiring businesses to continuously adapt and innovate. By understanding the dynamics of supply and demand, market structures, competitive strategies, and consumer behavior, businesses can navigate these environments effectively. Embracing innovation, leveraging technology, and adopting a customer-centric approach are essential for maintaining a competitive edge. As globalization and technological advancements continue to evolve, businesses must remain agile and responsive to stay ahead in the ever-changing competitive landscape. Building strong relationships with stakeholders is another critical aspect of thriving in competitive markets. Stakeholders include not only customers but also employees, suppliers, investors, and the community. By nurturing these relationships, businesses can create a supportive ecosystem that enhances their competitive position.

Goals and Structure of the Book

Every successful journey begins with a clear destination and a well-charted path. This book is designed to be your guide through the intricate landscape of competitive markets, offering insights, strategies, and practical advice to help your business not only navigate but thrive in such environments. The goals and structure of this book are meticulously crafted to provide a comprehensive understanding of competitive markets, blending theoretical knowledge with actionable strategies.

The primary goal of this book is to demystify the complexities of competitive markets, making them accessible and understandable. Competitive markets are often perceived as daunting arenas where only the strongest survive. However, with the right knowledge and tools, any business can find its niche and excel. This book aims to equip you with the insights needed to understand market dynamics, recognize opportunities, and implement strategies that foster growth and sustainability.

Understanding the competitive landscape is crucial for any business aiming to succeed. This book delves into the fundamental concepts of supply and demand, exploring how these forces shape market conditions and influence business decisions. By grasping these basics, you can better anticipate market trends and make informed decisions that align with your business goals. Additionally, the book examines various market structures, from perfect competition to monopolies, providing a framework to identify where your business fits within the broader market context and how to leverage this position effectively.

A critical aspect of thriving in competitive markets is the development and implementation of effective competitive strategies. This book outlines several key strategies, including cost leadership, differentiation, and focus strategies, explaining how each can be employed to gain a competitive edge. Cost leadership involves becoming the lowest-cost producer in your industry, allowing you to offer competitive pricing without sacrificing profitability. Differentiation focuses on creating unique products or services that stand out from the competition, while focus strategies target specific market segments with tailored offerings. By understanding and applying these strategies, you can position your business to attract and retain customers, even in the most competitive environments.

Consumer behavior is another focal point of this book. Understanding what drives consumer decisions, how preferences evolve, and the factors that influence purchasing behavior can give your business a significant advantage. This book explores various aspects of consumer behavior, from psychological influences to cultural trends, and provides practical advice on how to align your offerings with consumer needs and desires. By staying attuned to your customers, you can create products and services that resonate deeply, fostering loyalty and driving repeat business.

Innovation is the lifeblood of competitive markets. This book emphasizes the importance of continuous improvement and the development of new products and services. Innovation can take many forms, from technological advancements to process improvements and new business models. The book provides insights into how to foster a culture of innovation within your organization, encouraging creativity and experimentation. By staying ahead of market trends and continuously seeking ways to improve, your business can maintain a competitive edge and respond effectively to changing market conditions.

Globalization and technological advancements have transformed competitive markets, creating both opportunities and challenges. This book examines the impact of globalization, exploring how businesses can expand their reach, enter new markets, and compete on a global scale. It also delves into the role of technology, highlighting how digital transformation, automation, and the internet have reshaped industries and created new avenues for growth. By leveraging globalization and technology, your business can tap into new customer bases, streamline operations, and enhance competitiveness.

Building strong relationships with stakeholders is essential for long-term success in competitive markets. This book discusses the importance of nurturing relationships with customers, employees, suppliers, investors, and the community. By fostering trust and collaboration, you can create a supportive ecosystem that enhances your business's resilience and adaptability. The book provides practical advice on how to engage with stakeholders effectively, from employee engagement initiatives to supplier partnerships and investor relations. By prioritizing stakeholder relationships, your business can build a solid foundation for sustainable growth.

Marketing and brand positioning are critical components of success in competitive markets. This book explores various marketing strategies, from traditional advertising to digital marketing, social media, and content marketing. It emphasizes the importance of creating a strong brand identity that resonates with your target audience and differentiates your business from competitors. Effective branding involves more than just logos and slogans; it's about creating a compelling narrative that reflects your values and connects with customers on an emotional level. By crafting a powerful brand and implementing strategic marketing initiatives, your business can enhance visibility, attract new customers, and build long-term loyalty.

Pricing strategies are another key topic covered in this book. Pricing can significantly impact your business's competitiveness and profitability. The book explores various pricing strategies, including dynamic pricing, penetration pricing, and premium pricing, explaining how each can be used to achieve different business objectives. By understanding the principles of effective pricing, you can set prices that attract customers, maximize revenue, and respond to competitive pressures. The book also discusses the role of data analytics in pricing strategy, highlighting how advanced tools can provide insights into consumer behavior and market trends, enabling more informed pricing decisions.

Finally, this book emphasizes the importance of strategic planning and continuous assessment. Competitive markets are dynamic, and businesses must remain agile and responsive to succeed. The book provides frameworks for strategic planning, such as SWOT analysis and Porter's Five Forces, to help you assess your business's strengths, weaknesses, opportunities, and threats. It also discusses the importance of regular performance evaluations and market analysis, encouraging a proactive approach to strategy development. By continuously assessing your business's performance and adjusting strategies based on data and insights, you can stay aligned with market demands and maintain a competitive edge.

In summary, this book is designed to be a comprehensive guide to navigating competitive markets. It aims to demystify complex concepts, provide actionable strategies, and equip you with the knowledge and tools needed to succeed. By understanding market dynamics, developing effective strategies, fostering innovation, leveraging globalization and technology, building strong stakeholder relationships, crafting compelling marketing and branding initiatives, implementing effective pricing strategies, and engaging in strategic planning and continuous assessment, your business can thrive in even the most competitive environments. This journey through competitive markets is not just about survival; it's about seizing opportunities, driving growth, and achieving long-term success. Throughout this book, you will find a blend of theoretical insights and practical applications designed to provide a holistic understanding of competitive markets. The theoretical insights will offer you a solid foundation in market principles, while the practical applications will give you tools and strategies you can implement immediately.

Key Concepts and Definitions

Understanding the key concepts and definitions of competitive markets is essential for anyone looking to navigate this complex terrain. At its core, a competitive market is an economic system where multiple sellers offer similar products or services, and no single seller can control the market price. This environment encourages efficiency, innovation, and consumer choice, driving businesses to continuously improve their offerings.

One of the foundational concepts in competitive markets is supply and demand. Supply refers to the quantity of a product or service that businesses are willing to sell at various price points, while demand is the quantity that consumers are willing to purchase at those prices. The intersection of supply and demand determines the market price. When demand exceeds supply, prices tend to rise, attracting more producers to the market until equilibrium is reached. Conversely, when supply exceeds demand, prices fall, prompting some producers to exit the market or reduce production.

Market structures play a critical role in shaping competitive dynamics. There are four primary types of market structures: perfect competition, monopolistic competition, oligopoly, and monopoly. Perfect competition is characterized by many small firms, identical products, and easy entry and exit from the market. In this idealized scenario, no single firm can influence the market price, and all participants are price takers. Monopolistic competition, on the other hand, involves many firms offering differentiated products. While firms have some control over their prices, the presence of close substitutes limits their pricing power.

An oligopoly is a market structure dominated by a few large firms, each of which has significant control over market prices. These firms often engage in strategic interactions, such as price fixing or collusion, to maintain their market positions. Finally, a monopoly exists when a single firm controls the entire market for a particular product or service. This firm can set prices without concern for competition, often leading to higher prices and reduced consumer choice.

Barriers to entry are factors that make it difficult for new firms to enter a market. These barriers can be structural, such as high startup costs, or strategic, like aggressive tactics by existing firms to deter newcomers. Understanding these barriers is crucial for assessing the competitive landscape and identifying opportunities for market entry. High barriers to entry protect established firms but also stifle innovation and limit consumer options.

Consumer behavior is another essential concept in competitive markets. This field examines how individuals make purchasing decisions, influenced by factors such as preferences, income, and the prices of related goods. Behavioral economics has expanded our understanding by highlighting how cognitive biases and heuristics can affect consumer choices. For example, the anchoring effect can cause consumers to rely too heavily on the first piece of information they encounter, skewing their perception of value.

Price elasticity of demand measures how sensitive the quantity demanded of a product is to changes in its price. If demand is elastic, a small change in price leads to a significant change in quantity demanded. Conversely, if demand is inelastic, quantity demanded is relatively insensitive to price changes. Understanding price elasticity helps businesses set prices that maximize revenue and profit. For instance, luxury goods often have elastic demand, while necessities like food and medicine tend to have inelastic demand.

Competitive advantage is the unique value a company offers that sets it apart from its competitors. This advantage can be derived from various sources, such as superior technology, brand reputation, or cost efficiency. Companies strive to develop and sustain competitive advantages to attract and retain customers. Michael Porter's framework identifies two main types of competitive advantage: cost leadership and differentiation. Cost leadership involves becoming the lowest-cost producer in an industry, allowing a firm to offer lower prices or achieve higher margins. Differentiation, on the other hand, focuses on creating products or services that are perceived as unique and valuable by consumers.

Innovation is the process of developing new products, services, or processes that provide significant value to consumers and differentiate a company from its competitors. In competitive markets, innovation is vital for maintaining a competitive edge. Companies that fail to innovate risk becoming obsolete as more agile competitors introduce superior offerings. Innovation can take many forms, from incremental improvements to existing products to disruptive technologies that create entirely new markets.

Market segmentation is the practice of dividing a broad consumer or business market into subgroups of consumers based on shared characteristics. This allows companies to tailor their marketing efforts and product offerings to specific segments, improving their effectiveness and efficiency. Common segmentation criteria include demographics, psychographics, geographic location, and behavioral patterns. By understanding the unique needs and preferences of different segments, businesses can develop targeted strategies that resonate more deeply with their audience.

Positioning refers to how a company's product or service is perceived in the minds of consumers relative to competing offerings. Effective positioning involves identifying a unique value proposition and consistently communicating it through branding, marketing, and customer interactions. Positioning strategies can focus on attributes such as quality, price, convenience, or innovation. The goal is to create a distinct and favorable image that differentiates the product from competitors and aligns with the target market's needs.

Value chain analysis is a tool used to examine the activities a company performs to deliver a product or service, identifying areas where value can be added or costs can be reduced. The value chain includes primary activities such as inbound logistics, operations, outbound logistics, marketing and sales, and service, as well as support activities like procurement, technology development, human resource management, and firm infrastructure. By analyzing each component of the value chain, companies can identify opportunities for improving efficiency, enhancing product quality, and creating value for customers.

Market share is a measure of a company's sales relative to the total sales of all firms in the industry. It provides an indication of a company's competitiveness and market position. Increasing market share is often a key objective for businesses, as it can lead to economies of scale, greater brand recognition, and increased bargaining power with suppliers and customers. However, achieving higher market share requires a deep understanding of market dynamics, competitive strategies, and consumer behavior.

Economies of scale refer to the cost advantages that a company can achieve by increasing its production volume. As production scales up, the average cost per unit typically decreases due to factors such as more efficient use of resources, spreading fixed costs over a larger number of units, and improved bargaining power with suppliers. Economies of scale can provide a significant competitive advantage, allowing companies to offer lower prices or achieve higher margins. However, they also require substantial investment and efficient management of production processes.

Lastly, strategic alliances are partnerships between companies that collaborate to achieve common goals while remaining independent entities. These alliances can take various forms, such as joint ventures, licensing agreements, or research and development partnerships. Strategic alliances allow companies to combine resources, share risks, and access new markets more effectively than they could on their own. Successful alliances require clear objectives, mutual trust, and effective communication to ensure that both parties benefit from the collaboration.

In conclusion, understanding these key concepts and definitions is fundamental for navigating and succeeding in competitive markets. By grasping the principles of supply and demand, market structures, barriers to entry, consumer behavior, price elasticity, competitive advantage, innovation, market segmentation, positioning, value chain analysis, market share, economies of scale, and strategic alliances, businesses can develop informed strategies that enhance their competitiveness and drive long-term success. This comprehensive knowledge provides a solid foundation for making strategic decisions, identifying opportunities, and overcoming challenges in the dynamic world of competitive markets. Navigating the intricacies of competitive markets requires not just an understanding of key concepts but also the ability to apply these concepts effectively. This journey involves continuous learning, adaptation, and strategic thinking. As businesses seek to thrive in this environment, they must also consider several additional factors that influence their competitive position and overall market dynamics.

Chapter 2

The Foundations of Business Innovation

Understanding Innovation

Innovation is the lifeblood of any thriving business. It propels organizations forward, enabling them to adapt to changing markets, meet evolving customer demands, and stay ahead of competitors. At its core, innovation is about finding novel solutions to existing problems or creating entirely new value propositions that redefine industries. Understanding innovation requires a deep dive into its various forms, the processes that drive it, and the cultural and strategic frameworks that support it.

Innovation can be broadly categorized into two types: incremental and radical. Incremental innovation involves making small, continuous improvements to existing products, services, or processes. These improvements may not be groundbreaking but collectively, they can significantly enhance performance, efficiency, and customer satisfaction. For example, a software company might regularly release updates that add new features or improve usability, keeping their product relevant and competitive.

Radical innovation, on the other hand, entails developing entirely new products, services, or business models that disrupt existing markets or create new ones. This type of innovation is riskier and often requires significant investment in research and development. However, when successful, it can yield substantial rewards. Consider the impact of the smartphone: it revolutionized the way people communicate, access information, and conduct business, rendering many previous technologies obsolete.

The process of innovation often begins with identifying a problem or opportunity. This requires a keen understanding of market trends, customer needs, and technological advancements. Companies that excel in innovation invest in market research and maintain close connections with their customers to gather insights and feedback. Engaging with customers through surveys, focus groups, and social media can reveal pain points and unmet needs that can spark innovative ideas.

Once a potential opportunity is identified, the next step is ideation. This creative phase involves generating a wide array of ideas, without immediately worrying about their feasibility. Techniques such as brainstorming sessions, mind mapping, and design thinking workshops can help teams think outside the box and explore unconventional solutions. Encouraging a culture where all ideas are valued, and employees feel safe to take risks, is crucial for fostering creativity.

After generating a pool of ideas, the evaluation and selection phase begins. This involves assessing the feasibility, market potential, and strategic alignment of each idea. Criteria such as technical viability, cost, time to market, and potential return on investment are considered. It's essential to balance short-term gains with long-term strategic goals to ensure that the chosen innovations align with the company's vision and mission.

Prototyping and testing are critical steps in the innovation process. Developing prototypes allows companies to explore the practicality of their ideas and gather valuable feedback from users. This iterative process helps refine the concept, identify potential issues, and make necessary adjustments before full-scale implementation. Rapid prototyping techniques, such as 3D printing for physical products or wireframing for digital solutions, can accelerate this phase and reduce development costs.

Once a prototype is validated, the innovation moves into the implementation phase. This involves developing the final product or service, establishing production processes, and creating a go-to-market strategy. Effective project management and cross-functional collaboration are vital to ensure a smooth transition from concept to reality. Marketing and communication plans should be crafted to highlight the unique value proposition of the innovation and generate excitement among potential customers.

Innovation does not end with the launch of a new product or service. Continuous monitoring, feedback collection, and iteration are necessary to ensure ongoing success. Market conditions and customer preferences can change rapidly, and staying attuned to these shifts allows companies to make timely adjustments. Post-launch reviews and performance metrics help assess the impact of the innovation and identify opportunities for further improvement or new innovations.

Creating a culture of innovation within an organization is essential for sustaining long-term success. This culture is characterized by openness, collaboration, and a willingness to take calculated risks. Leaders play a pivotal role in fostering this environment by setting a clear vision, encouraging experimentation, and recognizing and rewarding innovative efforts. Providing employees with the resources, training, and autonomy to explore new ideas can unleash their creative potential.

Cross-functional teams are often more effective at driving innovation, as they bring diverse perspectives and expertise to the table. Collaboration between departments such as R&D, marketing, finance, and operations can lead to more holistic and market-ready solutions. Regularly scheduled innovation meetings or innovation hubs within the organization can facilitate these interactions and provide a dedicated space for creative thinking and problem-solving.

External partnerships and collaborations can also enhance a company's innovation capabilities. Engaging with universities, research institutions, startups, and other industry players can provide access to new technologies, knowledge, and markets. Open innovation, where companies actively seek and incorporate external ideas and solutions, can accelerate the innovation process and reduce development costs. For example, pharmaceutical companies often collaborate with academic researchers to discover new drugs and bring them to market more efficiently.

Innovation is not without its challenges. Resistance to change, fear of failure, and resource constraints can hinder innovative efforts. Overcoming these obstacles requires strong leadership, a clear innovation strategy, and effective change management practices. Communicating the benefits of innovation and involving employees in the process can help build buy-in and reduce resistance. Additionally, establishing a dedicated innovation budget and ensuring access to necessary resources can alleviate financial constraints.

Risk management is another critical aspect of innovation. While innovation inherently involves uncertainty, companies can mitigate risks through careful planning and scenario analysis. Diversifying the innovation portfolio, balancing high-risk projects with lower-risk incremental improvements, and having contingency plans in place can help manage potential downsides. Learning from failures and viewing them as opportunities for growth and learning is also essential for fostering a resilient innovation culture.

The role of technology in driving innovation cannot be overstated. Advances in digital technologies, such as artificial intelligence, big data, and the Internet of Things, are opening up new avenues for innovation across industries. Leveraging these technologies can enhance product development, optimize operations, and create new customer experiences. For instance, big data analytics can provide deeper insights into customer behavior, enabling more personalized and effective solutions.

Sustainability is increasingly becoming a key driver of innovation. As environmental concerns grow, companies are seeking ways to reduce their ecological footprint and develop sustainable products and practices. This shift towards sustainability is not only beneficial for the planet but also creates new business opportunities. Innovating in areas such as renewable energy, circular economy models, and eco-friendly materials can differentiate companies and attract environmentally conscious consumers.

Finally, measuring the impact of innovation is crucial for understanding its value and guiding future efforts. Key performance indicators (KPIs) such as revenue growth, market share, customer satisfaction, and time to market can provide insights into the effectiveness of innovation initiatives. Regularly reviewing these metrics and using them to inform strategic decisions helps ensure that innovation efforts are aligned with business goals and delivering the desired outcomes.

Innovation is a complex and multifaceted process that requires a strategic approach, a supportive culture, and a willingness to embrace change. By understanding the different types of innovation, the stages of the innovation process, and the factors that drive and support innovation, companies can harness its power to achieve sustainable growth and competitive advantage. As markets continue to evolve and new challenges arise, a commitment to innovation will be essential for staying relevant and thriving in the future. The journey of innovation extends beyond the initial phases of ideation and execution. It demands a continuous commitment to learning, adapting, and evolving. Companies that excel in innovation often embed it into their organizational DNA, making it a core part of their identity and operations.

Types of Innovation

Innovation is not a one-size-fits-all concept. It manifests in various forms, each with its own unique characteristics, processes, and impacts. Understanding the different types of innovation can help organizations tailor their strategies to achieve specific goals and navigate the complexities of the modern business environment. By recognizing the nuances between these types, companies can better allocate resources, manage risks, and maximize the benefits of their innovation efforts.

Incremental innovation is perhaps the most common type of innovation. It involves making small, continuous improvements to existing products, services, or processes. These improvements might not be revolutionary on their own, but over time, they can lead to significant enhancements in performance, efficiency, and customer satisfaction. For example, a car manufacturer might introduce incremental innovations such as better fuel efficiency, enhanced safety features, or improved infotainment systems in each new model. These changes keep the product competitive and meet evolving customer expectations without the high risks associated with more radical innovations.

Radical innovation, in contrast, represents a paradigm shift. It involves developing entirely new products, services, or business models that disrupt existing markets or create new ones. Radical innovations often leverage breakthrough technologies or novel approaches that render previous solutions obsolete.

The smartphone is a prime example of radical innovation. It didn't just improve upon existing mobile phones; it fundamentally changed how people communicate, access information, and interact with the digital world. Radical innovations carry higher risks and require substantial investments, but they also offer the potential for significant rewards and long-term competitive advantages.

Architectural innovation involves reconfiguring existing technologies or processes to create new markets or applications. This type of innovation doesn't necessarily introduce new components but rather reimagines how existing ones can be combined or used. A classic example is the transition from desktop computers to laptops. The core technology remained largely the same, but the new configuration enabled portability and flexibility, opening up new use cases and market segments. Architectural innovation can be a powerful way to leverage existing strengths while exploring new opportunities.

Disruptive innovation, a term popularized by Clayton Christensen, refers to innovations that initially target a niche market or underserved segment and gradually move upmarket, eventually displacing established competitors. Disruptive innovations often offer simpler, more affordable, or more accessible solutions compared to incumbent products. For instance, digital cameras started as low-quality alternatives to film cameras but eventually overtook the market as technology improved and consumer preferences shifted. Companies that recognize and embrace disruptive innovation can gain a foothold in emerging markets and challenge industry leaders.

Process innovation focuses on improving the methods and techniques used to produce goods or deliver services. This type of innovation aims to enhance efficiency, reduce costs, and improve quality. Lean manufacturing, pioneered by Toyota, is a prime example of process innovation. By streamlining production processes, minimizing waste, and optimizing resource use, Toyota revolutionized the automotive industry and set new standards for operational excellence. Process innovation can lead to significant competitive advantages by enabling companies to offer higher quality at lower prices or faster delivery times.

Product innovation, as the name suggests, involves creating new or significantly improved products. This type of innovation can be driven by technological advancements, changing consumer preferences, or competitive pressures. The introduction of electric vehicles (EVs) by companies like Tesla represents product innovation. EVs offer an alternative to traditional combustion engine vehicles, addressing environmental concerns and tapping into a growing market for sustainable transportation. Product innovation can help companies differentiate themselves, capture new markets, and drive growth.

Service innovation focuses on enhancing or creating new services to meet customer needs more effectively. This type of innovation often involves improving the customer experience, increasing convenience, or introducing new value propositions. For example, the rise of subscription-based models in industries like software, entertainment, and retail represents service innovation. Companies like Netflix and Spotify have transformed how people consume media by offering unlimited access to content through affordable subscriptions. Service innovation can foster customer loyalty, drive recurring revenue, and create competitive differentiation.

Business model innovation involves rethinking how a company creates, delivers, and captures value. This type of innovation can be particularly powerful because it can transform entire industries and unlock new revenue streams. A notable example is the rise of the sharing economy, exemplified by companies like Airbnb and Uber. These companies didn't just create new products or services; they fundamentally changed the way people access accommodation and transportation by leveraging peer-to-peer networks and digital platforms. Business model innovation can open up new growth opportunities and enable companies to stay ahead of market disruptions.

Open innovation is a collaborative approach that involves leveraging external ideas, technologies, and resources to drive innovation. This type of innovation recognizes that valuable insights and solutions can come from outside the organization. Companies that embrace open innovation actively seek partnerships with startups, research institutions, and other external entities. For example, Procter & Gamble's Connect + Develop program invites external innovators to collaborate on product development, resulting in a more diverse and dynamic innovation pipeline. Open innovation can accelerate the innovation process, reduce costs, and enhance creativity by tapping into a broader pool of talent and ideas.

Sustainable innovation focuses on creating products, services, and processes that have a positive impact on the environment and society. This type of innovation addresses the growing demand for sustainable solutions and aligns with global efforts to combat climate change, reduce waste, and promote social responsibility. Companies that prioritize sustainable innovation can differentiate themselves, meet regulatory requirements, and appeal to environmentally conscious consumers. For instance, the development of biodegradable packaging materials and renewable energy solutions represents sustainable innovation. This approach not only contributes to a better world but also creates new market opportunities and enhances brand reputation.

Social innovation involves developing solutions that address social challenges and improve the well-being of communities. This type of innovation often focuses on issues such as education, healthcare, poverty alleviation, and social inclusion. Social enterprises and non-profit organizations are key drivers of social innovation, but for-profit companies can also play a significant role. For example, microfinance institutions like Grameen Bank have pioneered innovative financial services that provide low-income individuals with access to credit and financial resources, empowering them to improve their livelihoods. Social innovation can generate significant social impact while also creating sustainable business opportunities.

Frugal innovation, also known as "jugaad" innovation, involves creating cost-effective solutions that meet the needs of resource-constrained consumers. This type of innovation is particularly relevant in emerging markets, where affordability and accessibility are critical. Frugal innovation emphasizes simplicity, efficiency, and resourcefulness. For example, the development of portable, low-cost medical devices that can be used in remote or underserved areas represents frugal innovation. Companies that excel in frugal innovation can tap into vast markets with high demand for affordable solutions and drive inclusive growth.

Understanding the various types of innovation provides a comprehensive framework for companies to navigate the complex landscape of innovation. Each type offers unique opportunities and challenges, and organizations must carefully consider which types align with their strategic objectives, capabilities, and market conditions. By embracing a diverse approach to innovation, companies can build resilience, drive growth, and create lasting value in an ever-evolving business environment. The interconnected nature of these innovation types underscores the importance of a holistic approach. While each type has distinct characteristics, they often overlap and influence one another. For instance, a breakthrough in product innovation might necessitate changes in the business model to effectively commercialize the new product. Similarly, process innovations can enhance the efficiency of delivering new services, and architectural innovations can open up new possibilities for both products and services.

The Role of Creativity in Innovation

Creativity is the lifeblood of innovation. It is the spark that ignites new ideas and the engine that drives progress. Without creativity, innovation would stagnate, and progress would grind to a halt. But what exactly is creativity, and how does it fuel the innovation process? Understanding the intricate relationship between creativity and innovation can provide valuable insights for individuals and organizations striving to stay ahead in an ever-evolving landscape.

Creativity involves generating novel and valuable ideas. It's about seeing the world through a different lens, challenging the status quo, and imagining possibilities that others might overlook. It's a process that often requires stepping outside of conventional thinking and embracing risk and uncertainty. While creativity can be an innate talent, it can also be cultivated and nurtured through practice and the right environment.

One of the most profound examples of creativity driving innovation comes from the story of Steve Jobs and Apple. When Jobs returned to Apple in the late 1990s, the company was struggling. However, by fostering a culture that valued creativity and encouraged risk-taking, Jobs and his team developed the iMac, iPod, iPhone, and iPad—products that didn't just improve on existing technologies but redefined entire markets. Jobs's ability to think differently and his commitment to nurturing creativity within his team were pivotal in transforming Apple into one of the most innovative companies in the world.

Creativity is not confined to the realms of art and design; it is essential in all fields, including science, engineering, and business. For example, in the pharmaceutical industry, creative thinking is crucial for developing new drugs and treatments. Researchers must think beyond traditional approaches, exploring novel compounds and mechanisms to address complex diseases. The development of mRNA vaccines for COVID-19 is a testament to the power of creativity in scientific innovation. Scientists at companies like Pfizer and Moderna reimagined vaccine technology, leading to a rapid and effective response to a global crisis.

Fostering creativity within an organization requires a deliberate effort to create an environment that encourages experimentation and values diverse perspectives. It starts with leadership. Leaders must model creative thinking, be open to new ideas, and encourage their teams to take calculated risks. They must create a safe space where failure is seen as a learning opportunity rather than a setback. This shift in mindset can unlock tremendous creative potential within a team.

One practical way to foster creativity is to encourage collaboration across different disciplines and departments. When people with diverse backgrounds and expertise come together, they bring unique perspectives that can lead to innovative solutions. For instance, a team comprising engineers, marketers, and designers might approach a problem from different angles, leading to a more holistic and creative solution. This interdisciplinary approach was exemplified by the creation of the original Macintosh computer, where software engineers, hardware engineers, and designers worked closely to create a product that was both functional and aesthetically pleasing.

Another key factor in nurturing creativity is providing the right tools and resources. This can include access to cutting-edge technology, training programs, and spaces designed to inspire creative thinking. Google's office spaces, for example, are designed to foster creativity and collaboration, with open workspaces, colorful decor, and areas for relaxation and play. These elements help create an environment where employees feel inspired and empowered to think creatively.

Time is also a critical resource for creativity. Innovation often requires periods of uninterrupted focus, where individuals can immerse themselves in deep thinking and exploration. Companies like 3M and Atlassian have implemented policies that allow employees to spend a portion of their work time on projects of their own choosing. This "20% time" policy has led to the development of some of the companies' most successful products, including Post-it Notes and the Trello project management tool.

However, creativity is not just about generating ideas; it's also about refining and implementing them. This requires a balance between divergent thinking—where many possibilities are explored—and convergent thinking—where the best ideas are selected and developed. Brainstorming sessions are a popular method for generating ideas, but they should be followed by critical evaluation and iteration to hone the most promising concepts.

For creativity to translate into innovation, it must be supported by a structured process that guides ideas from conception to implementation. This involves setting clear goals, establishing criteria for evaluating ideas, and defining the steps needed to bring an idea to market. The innovation funnel is a useful framework for managing this process, with stages for idea generation, screening, development, and commercialization. By providing a clear pathway for creative ideas to become tangible innovations, organizations can ensure that creativity leads to meaningful outcomes.

Moreover, creativity thrives in a culture that embraces diversity and inclusivity. Different cultural backgrounds, experiences, and perspectives can spark new ideas and challenge conventional thinking. Companies that prioritize diversity and inclusion are better positioned to tap into a wider range of creative potential. This can be seen in the success of global companies like IBM, which has long championed diversity as a driver of innovation.

In addition to fostering creativity within the organization, it's also important to look outside for inspiration. Engaging with customers, partners, and the broader community can provide fresh insights and ideas. Customer feedback, in particular, can be a rich source of inspiration, highlighting unmet needs and opportunities for innovation. Companies like Lego have successfully leveraged customer input to drive innovation, involving fans in the development of new products through initiatives like Lego Ideas.

Creativity is also closely linked to passion and motivation. When individuals are passionate about their work, they are more likely to invest the time and effort needed to develop creative solutions. Companies can nurture this passion by aligning work with employees' interests and values, providing opportunities for growth and development, and recognizing and celebrating creative achievements.

Finally, it's important to remember that creativity is a dynamic and ongoing process. It requires continuous effort and adaptation as new challenges and opportunities arise. Organizations must remain flexible and open to change, constantly seeking new ways to inspire and harness creativity.

In summary, creativity is a fundamental driver of innovation, essential for generating novel ideas and transforming them into valuable solutions. By creating an environment that encourages diverse perspectives, collaboration, risk-taking, and continuous learning, organizations can unlock their creative potential and drive sustained innovation. Through leadership commitment, structured processes, and a culture that values creativity, companies can turn creative ideas into groundbreaking innovations that shape the future. One way to stay ahead of the curve is to establish innovation labs or dedicated teams tasked with exploring new ideas and technologies. These innovation hubs can operate with a degree of autonomy, allowing them to experiment without the constraints of the day-to-day business operations. For example, Lockheed Martin's Skunk Works is famous for developing breakthrough technologies, from the

U-2 spy plane to the F-117 Nighthawk stealth fighter. By creating a space where creativity can flourish, organizations can cultivate an environment where groundbreaking innovations can take root.

Building an Innovative Culture

Innovation is not a mere outcome but a process deeply rooted in the culture of an organization. Building an innovative culture requires deliberate effort, strategic alignment, and a commitment to fostering an environment where creativity can flourish and innovative thinking is encouraged at all levels. This chapter delves into the essential elements and actionable steps necessary to cultivate a culture of innovation within an organization.

At the heart of an innovative culture lies the willingness to challenge the status quo. Organizations must create an atmosphere where questioning existing norms and proposing new ideas are not only accepted but welcomed. This begins with leadership, where executives and managers set the tone by demonstrating openness to new perspectives and a readiness to take calculated risks. When leaders visibly support and engage in innovative activities, they signal to the rest of the organization that innovation is a priority.

One of the fundamental steps in building an innovative culture is fostering a sense of psychological safety. Employees need to feel secure in expressing their ideas without fear of ridicule or retribution. This can be achieved through open communication channels, regular feedback sessions, and an emphasis on collaborative problem-solving. By encouraging a culture where all voices are heard and respected, organizations can tap into the diverse perspectives and ideas that drive innovation.

Creating a diverse and inclusive workplace is another critical component. Diversity of thought, background, and experience enriches the pool of ideas and fosters creative problem-solving. Organizations should strive to build teams with varied skill sets and perspectives, as this diversity can lead to more robust and innovative solutions. Inclusivity, on the other hand, ensures that all employees feel valued and empowered to contribute their unique insights.

Encouraging experimentation and tolerating failure are also vital. Innovation often involves venturing into uncharted territory, where not every idea will succeed. Organizations must create an environment where failure is seen as a learning opportunity rather than a setback. This can be facilitated by establishing processes for rapid prototyping and iterative development, allowing teams to test ideas quickly and learn from their outcomes. Celebrating both successes and failures as part of the innovation journey reinforces the message that taking risks is an integral part of the process.

Providing time and resources for creative thinking is essential. Many organizations have adopted policies that allocate a certain percentage of employees' time to work on passion projects or explore new ideas. This approach, popularized by companies like 3M and Google, has led to the development of breakthrough products and services. By giving employees the freedom to pursue their interests, organizations can unlock latent creativity and drive innovation.

Leadership plays a pivotal role in fostering an innovative culture. Leaders must not only advocate for innovation but also actively participate in it. This means being visible champions of new initiatives, providing the necessary resources, and removing obstacles that hinder creative efforts. Additionally, leaders should model the behaviors they wish to see in their teams, such as curiosity, openness to new ideas, and resilience in the face of setbacks.

Investing in continuous learning and development is another key strategy. Innovation thrives in environments where employees have access to ongoing education and skill-building opportunities. Organizations should offer training programs, workshops, and access to external resources that help employees stay abreast of the latest trends and technologies. Encouraging cross-functional collaboration and knowledge sharing further enhances the collective expertise and innovative capacity of the organization.

Recognizing and rewarding innovation is crucial to sustaining an innovative culture. Organizations should establish recognition programs that celebrate creative efforts and achievements. This can range from formal awards and incentives to informal acknowledgments in team meetings. By highlighting and rewarding innovative behavior, organizations reinforce the importance of innovation and motivate employees to continue pushing boundaries.

Creating physical and virtual spaces that inspire creativity can also have a significant impact. Work environments designed to foster collaboration and creativity can stimulate innovative thinking. This might include open-plan offices, dedicated brainstorming areas, or virtual collaboration tools that enable teams to share ideas and work together seamlessly. The design of these spaces should reflect the organization's commitment to innovation and provide the flexibility needed for various types of creative activities.

Building an innovative culture also requires aligning organizational structures and processes with innovation goals. This means creating flexible and adaptive structures that allow for quick decision-making and the rapid deployment of resources. Traditional hierarchical models can often stifle creativity; instead, organizations should explore more agile and decentralized structures that empower teams to take initiative and innovate.

Storytelling can be a powerful tool in embedding innovation into the organizational culture. Sharing stories of past innovation successes and the journeys behind them can inspire and motivate employees. These narratives highlight the impact of innovation and demonstrate that creative efforts can lead to significant achievements. Leaders can use storytelling to communicate the vision and values of the organization, reinforcing the importance of innovation in achieving long-term goals.

Engaging with external partners and the broader community can also contribute to building an innovative culture. Collaborating with startups, academic institutions, and industry networks can bring fresh ideas and perspectives into the organization. These external partnerships can act as catalysts for innovation, providing access to new technologies, methodologies, and market insights.

Finally, measuring and evaluating innovation efforts is essential for continuous improvement. Organizations should establish metrics and key performance indicators (KPIs) that track innovation activities and their outcomes. Regularly reviewing these metrics helps identify areas for improvement and ensures that innovation remains aligned with strategic objectives. By systematically assessing the impact of innovation initiatives, organizations can refine their approaches and sustain momentum.

In summary, building an innovative culture is a multifaceted endeavor that requires a holistic approach. It involves creating an environment where creativity is nurtured, risks are taken, and diverse perspectives are valued. Leadership commitment, psychological safety, continuous learning, and recognition are among the key elements that contribute to a thriving culture of innovation. By embedding these principles into the fabric of the organization, companies can foster an innovative mindset that drives sustained growth and competitive advantage. Organizations must also be vigilant in maintaining the innovative culture they have built. It is easy for initial excitement and momentum to wane over time, leading to stagnation. To prevent this, companies should regularly revisit and renew their commitment to innovation. This can involve periodic reviews of innovation strategies, refreshing training programs, and continuously seeking new sources of inspiration.

Case Studies of Foundational Innovations

When we consider the leaps in progress that have shaped our world, foundational innovations often stand out as the pivotal moments where industries transformed and new paradigms were established. These case studies of foundational innovations provide invaluable lessons for understanding how groundbreaking ideas take root and flourish.

One of the most iconic examples of foundational innovation is the advent of the personal computer (PC). In the late 1970s and early 1980s, computing was largely confined to large, complex machines used by businesses and universities. The notion of a computer in every home seemed far-fetched. However, visionaries like Steve Jobs and Steve Wozniak of Apple, and Bill Gates and Paul Allen of Microsoft, saw the potential for personal computing to revolutionize everyday life. Apple's introduction of the Apple II in 1977, followed by IBM's PC in 1981, marked the beginning of the personal computer era. These innovations were not just about hardware; they involved creating user-friendly software, developing new business models, and fostering a burgeoning ecosystem of developers and applications. The ripple effects of this innovation are still felt today, as personal computing has become integral to virtually every aspect of modern life.

Another seminal innovation that reshaped an industry is the invention of the assembly line by Henry Ford. In the early 20th century, automobiles were luxury items, handcrafted and expensive. Ford's introduction of the moving assembly line in 1913 revolutionized manufacturing by significantly reducing the time and cost of production. This innovation was rooted in the principle of breaking down complex tasks into simpler, repetitive actions that could be performed by workers with minimal training. The impact was profound: the Model T, once a luxury item, became affordable for the average American. Ford's assembly line not only transformed the automotive industry but also set a precedent for mass production techniques that have been adopted across various sectors.

The development of the internet is perhaps one of the most transformative foundational innovations of the late 20th century. Initially conceived as a project to enable communication between researchers and the military, the internet's potential for broader applications quickly became apparent. The launch of the World Wide Web by Tim Berners-Lee in 1991 democratized access to information and laid the groundwork for the digital revolution. The internet has since evolved into a global platform for communication, commerce, and entertainment. Companies like Amazon, Google, and Facebook have built entire industries on this foundation, fundamentally altering how we interact with the world and each other. The internet's role in fostering innovation is unparalleled, providing a fertile ground for countless new ideas and business models.

Another noteworthy case study is the innovation of containerization in the shipping industry. Prior to the 1950s, goods were loaded and unloaded from ships in a labor-intensive and time-consuming process known as break-bulk shipping. Malcolm McLean, a trucking entrepreneur, revolutionized the industry by introducing standardized containers that could be easily transferred between ships, trucks, and trains. This innovation drastically reduced shipping times and costs, enabling the global supply chains we rely on today. Containerization not only transformed the shipping industry but also played a pivotal role in the globalization of trade, making it possible to efficiently transport goods across vast distances.

The field of healthcare has also seen foundational innovations that have had profound impacts. The development of antibiotics in the early 20th century revolutionized medicine by providing effective treatments for bacterial infections that were once deadly. Alexander Fleming's discovery of penicillin in 1928, followed by its mass production during World War II, marked the beginning of the antibiotic era. This innovation saved countless lives and paved the way for the development of a wide range of antibiotics that continue to be critical in modern medicine. The impact of antibiotics extends beyond individual health, influencing public health policies and the overall approach to treating infectious diseases.

In the realm of energy, the development of nuclear power stands out as a foundational innovation. The discovery of nuclear fission in the 1930s and the subsequent development of nuclear reactors provided a new, powerful source of energy. The first commercial nuclear power plant, opened in Shippingport, Pennsylvania in 1958, demonstrated the potential of nuclear energy to provide large-scale, low-carbon power. While nuclear power has faced challenges related to safety and waste disposal, its role in providing a significant portion of the world's electricity cannot be understated. The innovation in nuclear technology has also spurred advancements in other fields, including medicine and space exploration.

Another transformative innovation is the creation of the smartphone. The introduction of the iPhone by Apple in 2007 marked a significant shift in mobile technology. By combining a phone, a music player, and an internet device in one sleek package, the iPhone set a new standard for what mobile devices could be. This innovation was not just about hardware; it involved creating a user-friendly interface and an ecosystem of applications that could be easily downloaded and used. The smartphone has since become an indispensable tool in our daily lives, fundamentally changing how we communicate, work, and entertain ourselves.

The financial industry has also experienced foundational innovations, particularly with the advent of blockchain technology. Initially developed as the underlying technology for Bitcoin, blockchain has the potential to revolutionize the way transactions are conducted and recorded. By providing a decentralized, secure, and transparent method for recording transactions, blockchain technology can reduce the need for intermediaries and increase trust in digital transactions. The implications of blockchain extend beyond cryptocurrencies, with potential applications in supply chain management, voting systems, and digital identity verification.

One more foundational innovation that has had a significant impact is the development of renewable energy technologies. Wind, solar, and hydroelectric power have transformed the energy landscape by providing sustainable alternatives to fossil fuels. Advances in solar panel efficiency, wind turbine technology, and energy storage solutions have made renewable energy more viable and cost-effective. These innovations are crucial in addressing the global challenge of climate change and reducing our reliance on non-renewable energy sources.

These case studies of foundational innovations illustrate the profound and far-reaching impacts that groundbreaking ideas can have on various industries and aspects of society. Each innovation required vision, perseverance, and the ability to see beyond the immediate challenges to the broader potential. They also highlight the importance of creating environments that foster creativity, support risk-taking, and enable the translation of bold ideas into reality. By understanding the factors that contributed to these successful innovations, organizations and individuals can better navigate the complexities of innovation and drive meaningful progress in their own fields.

Chapter 3
Market Analysis and Trends

Identifying Market Needs

Identifying market needs is a foundational step for any successful business venture. This process involves understanding what consumers want, what gaps exist in the market, and how a product or service can meet those needs better than existing solutions. The ability to accurately identify and respond to market needs can be the difference between a thriving business and one that fails to gain traction.

A critical first step in identifying market needs is conducting thorough market research. This involves gathering data from a variety of sources to gain insight into consumer behavior and preferences. Surveys, focus groups, and interviews are traditional methods that can yield valuable qualitative data. For instance, a startup aiming to launch a new health drink might conduct surveys to understand consumer preferences regarding taste, packaging, and health benefits. They might also hold focus groups to discuss perceptions of existing products and identify unfulfilled needs. These methods provide direct feedback from potential customers, allowing businesses to tailor their offerings more precisely.

Quantitative data is equally important. Market analysis reports, sales data, and demographic statistics can help identify trends and patterns. For example, analyzing sales data might reveal a growing demand for organic products, while demographic statistics might indicate a significant population segment that is underserved. Combining qualitative and quantitative data provides a comprehensive view of the market landscape, helping businesses identify where opportunities lie.

Understanding the competitive landscape is another crucial aspect. By analyzing competitors, businesses can identify gaps that they can exploit. This involves looking at competitors' products, pricing strategies, marketing tactics, and customer feedback. For instance, if a competitor's product receives consistent complaints about durability, this presents an opportunity to enter the market with a more durable alternative. Competitive analysis also helps businesses understand what works well and what doesn't, allowing them to learn from others' successes and mistakes.

Customer feedback is an invaluable resource for identifying market needs. Engaging with customers through social media, online reviews, and customer service interactions can provide real-time insights into their needs and pain points. For example, a company might notice a recurring theme in customer complaints about the complexity of using a product. This feedback can guide the development of a more user-friendly version. Moreover, actively seeking customer feedback demonstrates that a business values its customers, fostering loyalty and trust.

Trends and innovations in the industry can also highlight emerging market needs. Staying abreast of technological advancements, regulatory changes, and cultural shifts can reveal new opportunities. For instance, the rise of sustainable and eco-friendly products reflects a growing consumer awareness of environmental issues. Companies that recognize and respond to these trends can position themselves as leaders in their industry. Attending industry conferences, networking with other professionals, and subscribing to trade publications are effective ways to keep up with industry developments.

Another method to identify market needs is through the use of personas. Personas are fictional characters created based on research to represent different user types. They help businesses empathize with their customers and understand their needs, preferences, and behaviors. For example, a tech company developing a new app might create personas for different types of users, such as a tech-savvy teenager, a busy professional, and a senior citizen. Each persona would have unique needs and challenges, guiding the development process to ensure the app meets a wide range of customer requirements.

Additionally, scenario planning can be a useful tool. This involves creating detailed narratives about potential future scenarios and exploring how these scenarios might impact market needs. For instance, a company might consider how an economic downturn would affect consumer spending or how a new technology could disrupt the market. By anticipating various possibilities, businesses can develop flexible strategies that allow them to adapt to changing market conditions.

Observing and analyzing customer behavior in real life can also provide insights. This can be done through ethnographic research, where researchers observe how people use products or services in their natural environment. For example, a furniture company might visit customers' homes to see how they interact with their products, revealing insights that surveys might miss. This method provides a deeper understanding of the context in which products are used and the real-life challenges customers face.

Collaborating with other businesses and organizations can also uncover market needs. Partnerships with companies in related industries, academic institutions, or research organizations can provide access to new perspectives and expertise. For example, a food company might collaborate with a health research institute to identify emerging dietary trends. These collaborations can lead to innovative solutions that address unmet needs in the market.

Once market needs have been identified, it's essential to validate these findings through testing and iteration. Developing prototypes or minimum viable products (MVPs) and testing them with a small group of users can provide valuable feedback and reveal whether the identified needs are being met. For instance, a startup might create a basic version of their app and release it to a select group of users to gather feedback on its functionality and usability. This iterative process allows for refining the product based on real-world feedback before a full-scale launch.

Effective communication of identified market needs within the organization is also crucial. Ensuring that all team members understand the target market and customer needs aligns efforts across departments, from product development to marketing and sales.

Regular meetings, detailed reports, and collaborative tools can facilitate this communication. For example, a shared document outlining key customer personas and their needs can be a valuable reference for the entire team.

Finally, it's important to recognize that market needs are not static. They evolve over time as new trends emerge, technologies advance, and consumer preferences change. Continuous market research and adaptability are essential for staying relevant. Businesses must remain vigilant, regularly revisiting their market research and adjusting their strategies accordingly. For instance, a company that initially identified a need for a specific health supplement might later find that consumer interest has shifted towards a different type of wellness product. Staying agile and responsive to these changes ensures long-term success.

Identifying market needs is a dynamic and ongoing process that requires a combination of research, analysis, and creativity. By understanding consumers' desires, monitoring industry trends, and staying engaged with customers, businesses can uncover valuable opportunities and develop products and services that truly meet market demands. This proactive approach not only drives business growth but also fosters innovation and customer satisfaction, creating a strong foundation for sustained success. Innovation plays a crucial role in identifying and responding to market needs. By fostering a culture of creativity and encouraging out-of-the-box thinking, businesses can develop unique solutions that stand out in the marketplace. Innovation doesn't always mean creating something entirely new; it often involves improving existing products or processes to better meet customer needs. For instance, a company in the tech industry might innovate by enhancing the features of an existing app to make it more intuitive and user-friendly, thus addressing previously unmet customer needs.

Analyzing Competitors

Analyzing competitors is a critical aspect of developing a successful business strategy. Understanding what your competitors are doing well, where they are falling short, and how they engage with their customers provides invaluable insights that can inform your own business decisions. This analysis not only helps in identifying market opportunities but also in avoiding potential pitfalls.

The first step in competitor analysis is identifying who your competitors are. This may seem straightforward, but it often requires a nuanced approach. Direct competitors are those who offer similar products or services to the same target market. For instance, if you run a coffee shop, other coffee shops in your area are your direct competitors. However, indirect competitors also play a significant role. These are businesses offering different products or services that fulfill the same customer need. Using the coffee shop example, a local bakery or a convenience store with a coffee station could be considered indirect competitors. It's essential to cast a wide net initially to ensure you don't overlook any potential competition.

Once you've identified your competitors, the next step is to gather as much information about them as possible. Start with their public-facing materials. This includes their websites, social media profiles, and press releases. Pay close attention to how they position themselves in the market, the key messages they use in their marketing, and the features they highlight in their products or services. Take note of their pricing strategies, promotional offers, and customer engagement tactics. For example, a competitor might emphasize their use of organic ingredients or their commitment to sustainability, which could be a significant selling point for environmentally conscious consumers.

Customer reviews and feedback are another valuable source of information. Sites like Yelp, Google Reviews, and industry-specific forums can provide insights into what customers like and dislike about your competitors' offerings. Look for patterns in the feedback. Are there recurring complaints about product quality, customer service, or delivery times? Conversely, are there consistent praises for particular features or aspects? For instance, if multiple reviews highlight that a competitor's product is durable but lacks aesthetic appeal, this could indicate an opportunity for you to offer a product that is both durable and visually appealing.

Competitive analysis should also include an evaluation of the competitors' strengths and weaknesses. Strengths are areas where the competitor excels and might include factors such as brand reputation, customer loyalty, or technological superiority. Weaknesses, on the other hand, are areas where the competitor is lacking. This could be poor customer service, limited product range, or high prices. Conducting a SWOT analysis (Strengths, Weaknesses, Opportunities, Threats) can provide a structured way to assess these elements. For example, a competitor might have a strong brand presence but suffer from frequent stockouts. This presents an opportunity for you to capture dissatisfied customers by ensuring reliable availability of your products.

Understanding the competitive landscape also involves analyzing the market positioning of each competitor. Market positioning refers to how a brand is perceived in the context of the competition. It involves identifying the unique value proposition that sets a competitor apart. For instance, one competitor might position itself as a luxury brand, targeting high-income consumers with premium pricing and exclusive features. Another might adopt a value-based approach, offering lower prices and appealing to cost-conscious customers. Mapping out the positioning of each competitor can help you identify gaps in the market that your business can fill. If no competitors are targeting mid-range consumers with high-quality but affordable products, this could be a lucrative opportunity.

Observing competitors' marketing and advertising strategies offers further insights. Analyze the channels they use, the frequency and timing of their campaigns, and the messaging they employ. For instance, if a competitor is highly active on Instagram and engages influencers to promote their products, this could indicate that their target audience is young and digitally savvy. Understanding these strategies allows you to identify effective tactics that you can adopt or improve upon. Additionally, it can reveal areas where your competitors might be underperforming, such as neglecting certain social media platforms or failing to engage in content marketing.

Another important aspect of competitor analysis is studying their business operations and supply chain. This includes examining how they source their materials, manage their inventory, and handle logistics. For example, a competitor might have a streamlined supply chain that allows them to offer lower prices or faster delivery times. Alternatively, they might face challenges such as supply shortages or high production costs. Understanding these operational aspects can help you identify ways to optimize your own processes and gain a competitive edge.

Financial performance provides a quantitative measure of a competitor's success and stability. Publicly traded companies are required to disclose financial information, which can be a goldmine for competitor analysis. Key metrics to consider include revenue, profit margins, growth rates, and market share. For instance, if a competitor has been experiencing rapid revenue growth, it might indicate strong market demand for their products. Conversely, declining profits could signal underlying issues such as rising costs or decreasing sales. Even for privately held companies, you can often find financial information through industry reports, market research firms, or business news articles.

Innovation and product development are areas where competitors can significantly impact the market.

Keeping an eye on new product launches, technological advancements, and R&D activities can provide insights into future trends and potential disruptions. For example, if a competitor is investing heavily in developing eco-friendly packaging, this could signal a growing market demand for sustainable products. By staying informed about these innovations, you can anticipate market shifts and adapt your strategy accordingly.

Strategic partnerships and alliances are another aspect to consider. Competitors often collaborate with other businesses, organizations, or even competitors to enhance their offerings or expand their market reach. For instance, a competitor might partner with a popular brand to co-develop a new product line or collaborate with a tech company to integrate advanced features into their products. Understanding these partnerships can provide insights into the strategic direction of your competitors and highlight potential opportunities for your own business.

Lastly, it's crucial to continuously monitor and update your competitor analysis. The business landscape is dynamic, with new competitors entering the market, existing ones evolving, and market conditions changing. Regularly reviewing and updating your analysis ensures that you remain informed about the latest developments and can adjust your strategy as needed. This ongoing process helps you stay agile and responsive to competitive pressures, allowing you to maintain a strong position in the market.

One effective way to keep your competitor analysis up-to-date is by setting up alerts and notifications. Tools like Google Alerts can notify you whenever your competitors are mentioned in the news or online, providing real-time updates on their activities. Additionally, subscribing to industry newsletters, joining professional networks, and attending trade shows can help you stay informed about the latest trends and competitive dynamics.

Analyzing competitors is an essential practice for any business looking to gain a competitive edge. By thoroughly understanding your competitors' strengths, weaknesses, strategies, and market positioning, you can make informed decisions that enhance your own business performance. This comprehensive approach not only helps you identify opportunities and mitigate risks but also fosters a deeper understanding of the market landscape, ultimately contributing to long-term success. To make your competitor analysis even more actionable, it's beneficial to synthesize all the gathered information into a comprehensive report. This report should highlight key insights and recommend specific actions based on your findings. Here's a detailed approach to crafting such a report and implementing its insights effectively.

Trend Spotting and Forecasting

Trend spotting and forecasting are essential skills for anyone looking to stay ahead in a rapidly changing market. Recognizing emerging trends before they become mainstream can provide a significant competitive edge, allowing businesses to innovate, adapt, and capitalize on new opportunities. To effectively spot and forecast trends, it's crucial to employ a combination of observation, analysis, and strategic thinking.

One of the most effective ways to spot trends is by immersing yourself in the industry and its related fields. Attend industry conferences, trade shows, and seminars to gather insights from experts and peers. These events are often where new ideas and technologies are first introduced, providing a glimpse into the future of the industry. For example, a technology conference might showcase the latest advancements in artificial intelligence, hinting at future applications and market shifts.

Networking is another powerful tool for trend spotting. Building relationships with industry insiders, thought leaders, and influencers can provide access to valuable information and perspectives. Engage in conversations, ask questions, and listen to what others are saying about emerging trends. These interactions can reveal patterns and shifts that may not be immediately apparent from a distance. For instance, a casual conversation with a supplier might uncover a new manufacturing technique that could revolutionize production processes.

Staying informed through a variety of sources is also crucial. Subscribe to industry publications, follow relevant blogs, and join online forums and communities. Social media platforms like Twitter, LinkedIn, and Instagram can be particularly useful for real-time updates and discussions. Following key hashtags and thought leaders can expose you to the latest developments and emerging trends. For instance, monitoring hashtags related to sustainability might reveal a growing consumer demand for eco-friendly products.

Data analysis plays a critical role in trend spotting and forecasting. Collecting and analyzing data from various sources can help identify patterns and trends. This could include sales data, consumer behavior, market research reports, and social media analytics. For instance, analyzing sales trends over time might reveal seasonal patterns or shifts in consumer preferences. Similarly, social media analytics can provide insights into the topics and products gaining traction among consumers.

Technology can enhance your trend-spotting efforts. Tools like Google Trends, for example, allow you to track the popularity of search terms over time, revealing shifts in consumer interest. Similarly, sentiment analysis tools can analyze social media posts, reviews, and other text data to gauge public opinion and identify emerging trends. For instance, a sudden increase in positive sentiment around a new product category could indicate a burgeoning trend.

Trend forecasting involves predicting how identified trends will evolve and impact the market in the future. This requires a deep understanding of the industry, consumer behavior, and external factors such as economic conditions and technological advancements. Scenario planning is a useful technique for trend forecasting. This involves envisioning different future scenarios based on current trends and analyzing their potential impacts on your business. For instance, if a trend towards remote work continues, how might that affect demand for office space or commuter services?

Engaging with early adopters and innovators can provide valuable insights into future trends. These individuals and organizations are often the first to embrace new technologies and ideas, providing a preview of what might become mainstream. Observing their behaviors and preferences can offer clues about the direction of the market. For example, if tech-savvy consumers are rapidly adopting a new gadget, it might indicate a broader trend that will soon follow.

Consumer surveys and feedback are another important source of information for trend forecasting. Directly asking your customers about their preferences, needs, and expectations can provide actionable insights. Conducting regular surveys and focus groups can help you stay attuned to changing consumer sentiments and anticipate future trends. For instance, if a significant portion of your customer base expresses interest in sustainable products, this could signal a growing trend towards eco-conscious consumption.

Historical analysis can also inform trend forecasting. Examining past trends and their trajectories can provide context and help you understand how similar trends might unfold in the future. For example, studying the adoption curve of previous technological innovations can offer insights into the likely pace and pattern of adoption for new technologies. Additionally, understanding the factors that influenced past trends can help you identify potential drivers of future trends.

Trend forecasting is not an exact science, and it's important to remain flexible and adaptable. The market is influenced by a multitude of factors, many of which are unpredictable. Being open to new information and willing to adjust your forecasts as needed is crucial. Regularly reviewing and updating your trend forecasts ensures they remain relevant and accurate. For instance, if a new regulatory change is announced, it might necessitate a revision of your forecasts to account for its potential impact.

Implementing identified trends into your business strategy requires careful planning and execution. Start by evaluating the relevance and potential impact of each trend on your business. Not all trends will be applicable or beneficial, so it's important to prioritize those that align with your goals and capabilities. For example, a trend towards digital transformation might be highly relevant for a tech company but less so for a traditional manufacturing business.

Developing a strategic plan to leverage identified trends involves setting clear objectives, allocating resources, and defining actionable steps. This might include investing in new technologies, launching new products, or entering new markets. For instance, if your trend forecasting indicates a growing demand for plant-based foods, you might decide to develop a new line of plant-based products to capture this market opportunity.

Monitoring the progress and impact of your trend-based initiatives is essential for success. Establish key performance indicators (KPIs) to track the effectiveness of your strategies and make adjustments as needed. Regularly reviewing your progress against these KPIs ensures you stay on track and can quickly respond to any challenges or changes in the market.

For example, if sales of a new product line are not meeting expectations, analyzing the underlying reasons and making necessary adjustments can help improve performance.

Cultivating a culture of innovation within your organization is key to successfully spotting and leveraging trends. Encourage employees to stay informed about industry developments, share their insights, and experiment with new ideas. Creating an environment where innovation is valued and rewarded fosters a proactive approach to trend spotting and forecasting. For instance, hosting regular brainstorming sessions and innovation workshops can generate fresh ideas and keep your team engaged with emerging trends.

In conclusion, trend spotting and forecasting are dynamic processes that require a combination of observation, analysis, and strategic thinking. By staying informed, leveraging data, engaging with early adopters, and remaining adaptable, businesses can effectively identify and capitalize on emerging trends. This proactive approach not only helps you stay ahead of the competition but also drives innovation and growth, ensuring long-term success in a rapidly evolving market. To truly master trend spotting and forecasting, it's beneficial to integrate these practices into the core functions of your organization. This means embedding a forward-looking perspective into your company's culture, operations, and strategic planning processes. Here are some additional strategies to enhance your capabilities in this area.

Using Data to Drive Decisions

Data has become the cornerstone of contemporary decision-making, guiding businesses, governments, and individuals toward more informed choices. The ability to harness, interpret, and utilize data effectively can distinguish successful ventures from those that flounder. This chapter delves into the strategies and methodologies for using data to drive decisions, providing practical and actionable advice that beginners can implement to start making data-driven decisions.

To begin, it is essential to understand what constitutes data and its various forms. Data can be quantitative, such as sales numbers, website traffic, or financial figures, and qualitative, like customer feedback, user reviews, or interview transcripts. Each type of data offers unique insights and requires different approaches for analysis. Recognizing the kind of data at your disposal is the first step in leveraging it for decision-making.

The next critical aspect is data collection. Gathering accurate and relevant data is paramount. This process can involve various methods, such as surveys, web analytics, financial reports, social media monitoring, and more. Effective data collection hinges on setting clear objectives. What questions are you seeking to answer? What decisions are you looking to inform? Defining these goals will help focus your data collection efforts and ensure you gather the most pertinent information.

Once you have collected data, the next step is to clean and organize it. Raw data often contains errors, inconsistencies, and irrelevant information. Data cleaning involves checking for and correcting inaccuracies, dealing with missing values, and standardizing formats. For instance, if you have a dataset with dates in different formats, convert them into a consistent format to ensure accurate analysis. This step, though tedious, is crucial as it ensures the reliability of your data, which directly impacts the quality of your decisions.

With clean data in hand, it's time to analyze it. The analysis can take many forms, depending on the type of data and the questions you seek to answer. Statistical analysis, data visualization, and predictive modeling are some common techniques. Statistical analysis helps uncover trends, correlations, and patterns within the data. For example, you might use regression analysis to understand the relationship between advertising spend and sales revenue. Data visualization tools, like charts and graphs, can make complex data more understandable and highlight key insights in an easily digestible format. Predictive modeling, on the other hand, uses historical data to forecast future outcomes, aiding in proactive decision-making rather than reactive.

A crucial part of data analysis is identifying key performance indicators (KPIs). KPIs are metrics that reflect the performance and success of an organization or project. Choosing the right KPIs is vital, as they provide a focused lens through which to view your data. For instance, an e-commerce business might track KPIs such as conversion rate, average order value, and customer acquisition cost. Regularly monitoring these KPIs helps in making informed decisions and measuring the impact of those decisions over time.

Scenario analysis is another valuable technique in data-driven decision-making. This involves creating different scenarios based on varying assumptions and analyzing their potential outcomes. For example, a company might model the financial impact of entering a new market under different economic conditions. Scenario analysis allows decision-makers to anticipate possible challenges and opportunities, making them better prepared for future uncertainties.

It's also essential to cultivate a data-driven culture within your organization. This means encouraging and enabling employees at all levels to use data in their decision-making processes. Providing training on data literacy, investing in user-friendly data tools, and fostering an environment where data is openly shared and discussed can significantly enhance your organization's ability to make informed decisions. When everyone in the organization understands the value of data and feels empowered to use it, the collective decision-making power increases manifold.

One practical application of data-driven decision-making is in marketing. Marketers can use data to understand customer behavior, segment their audience, and tailor their strategies accordingly. For instance, analyzing website traffic data can reveal which pages are most popular and where users drop off, informing decisions on website design and content. Social media analytics can provide insights into what type of content resonates most with your audience, guiding your content creation and posting strategies. By continuously measuring and analyzing the performance of marketing campaigns, businesses can optimize their efforts for better results.

In finance, data-driven decision-making can enhance budgeting, forecasting, and investment strategies. Financial analysts use historical financial data to project future revenue and expenses, helping businesses plan and allocate resources more effectively. Investment decisions are also increasingly driven by data, with algorithms analyzing vast amounts of market data to identify trends and opportunities. This approach reduces the reliance on gut feeling and increases the likelihood of making profitable investments.

The healthcare sector also benefits significantly from data-driven decision-making. Patient data, such as medical history, treatment outcomes, and genetic information, can be analyzed to improve diagnosis and treatment plans. Predictive analytics can identify patients at high risk of developing certain conditions, enabling early intervention and better patient outcomes. Data can also drive operational decisions, such as optimizing staff schedules, managing inventory, and improving patient flow, ultimately enhancing the efficiency and effectiveness of healthcare delivery.

Despite its many advantages, data-driven decision-making is not without challenges. One common issue is data overload. With the vast amount of data available, it can be overwhelming to sift through and identify what is truly important. This is where prioritization and focus come in. Clearly defining your objectives and KPIs helps narrow down the data to what is most relevant, preventing you from getting lost in a sea of information.

Another challenge is ensuring data privacy and security. With increasing concerns over data breaches and misuse, it is crucial to handle data responsibly. This means implementing robust data protection measures, complying with relevant regulations, and being transparent with stakeholders about how their data is used. Building trust through ethical data practices is essential for maintaining a positive reputation and avoiding legal pitfalls.

Finally, it's important to recognize that data should inform decisions, not dictate them. While data provides valuable insights and can reduce uncertainty, it is not infallible. Context, experience, and intuition still play crucial roles in decision-making. The best decisions often come from a combination of data-driven insights and human judgment. By balancing these elements, you can make more holistic and effective decisions.

In conclusion, using data to drive decisions is a multifaceted process that involves collecting, cleaning, analyzing, and interpreting data to inform actions. It requires a clear understanding of your objectives, the right tools and techniques, and a culture that values and utilizes data. By following these principles, beginners can start making more informed decisions, leading to better outcomes and a competitive edge in their respective fields. Building a framework for data-driven decision-making within an organization also involves continuous improvement and adaptation. The landscape of data and technology evolves rapidly, and staying updated with the latest tools and methodologies is crucial. Regularly reviewing your data practices and incorporating new advancements can enhance your decision-making capabilities and ensure you remain competitive.

Understanding Customer Behavior

Understanding customer behavior is crucial for any business aiming to thrive in a competitive market. It involves observing, analyzing, and interpreting the actions and decisions of consumers to tailor products, services, and marketing efforts effectively. By delving into the motivations behind customer choices, businesses can enhance customer satisfaction, loyalty, and ultimately, profitability.

At the heart of understanding customer behavior is the concept of the customer journey. This journey encompasses all the touchpoints and interactions a customer has with a brand, from initial awareness to post-purchase engagement. Mapping out the customer journey helps in identifying key moments of influence and areas where improvements can be made. For instance, a retail business might discover that customers frequently abandon their shopping carts at the payment stage. By analyzing this behavior, the business can streamline the checkout process to reduce friction and increase conversions.

Data plays a pivotal role in understanding customer behavior. Collecting and analyzing data from various sources, such as website analytics, social media, sales transactions, and customer feedback, provides valuable insights into how customers interact with a brand. For example, website analytics can reveal which pages attract the most visitors, how long they stay, and what actions they take. Social media data can show which content resonates most with the audience, while sales data can highlight buying patterns and preferences.

Segmentation is a powerful technique for gaining deeper insights into customer behavior. By dividing the customer base into distinct groups based on characteristics such as demographics, purchasing behavior, or psychographics, businesses can tailor their strategies to meet the specific needs of each segment. For instance, a company might identify a segment of tech-savvy millennials who prefer online shopping and are responsive to digital marketing campaigns. By targeting this segment with personalized offers and content, the company can increase engagement and sales.

Psychographics, which include attitudes, values, interests, and lifestyles, offer another layer of understanding beyond basic demographic data. Understanding the underlying motivations and desires of customers can help businesses create more compelling value propositions. For example, a fitness brand might appeal to health-conscious individuals by emphasizing the quality and benefits of their products in promoting a healthy lifestyle. By aligning marketing messages with the values and interests of the target audience, businesses can create a stronger emotional connection and drive brand loyalty.

Customer feedback is an invaluable resource for understanding behavior. Direct feedback through surveys, interviews, and reviews provides firsthand insights into customer experiences and perceptions.

For example, a restaurant can use feedback from diners to improve its menu, service, and ambiance. By actively seeking and responding to feedback, businesses demonstrate that they value their customers' opinions, fostering a sense of trust and loyalty.

Behavioral analysis tools, such as heatmaps and session recordings, offer a granular view of how customers interact with digital platforms. Heatmaps show where users click, scroll, and spend the most time on a webpage, helping businesses identify which elements capture attention and which may need adjustments. Session recordings provide a playback of user interactions, revealing pain points and areas where users may encounter difficulties. By analyzing these behaviors, businesses can optimize their websites and apps to enhance user experience and drive conversions.

Predictive analytics is another powerful tool for understanding and anticipating customer behavior. By analyzing historical data, businesses can identify patterns and trends that predict future actions. For instance, an e-commerce company might use predictive analytics to forecast which products are likely to be popular during the holiday season. This allows the company to stock up on inventory and plan marketing campaigns accordingly. Predictive analytics can also help in identifying at-risk customers who may be likely to churn, enabling proactive retention strategies.

Understanding customer behavior also involves recognizing the influence of external factors. Economic conditions, cultural trends, technological advancements, and competitive actions can all impact customer decisions. For example, during an economic downturn, consumers may prioritize value and affordability, leading businesses to adjust their pricing strategies and emphasize cost-effective solutions. Staying attuned to these external factors allows businesses to adapt their strategies in response to changing customer needs and preferences.

Storytelling is a powerful technique for connecting with customers on an emotional level. By sharing stories that resonate with their audience, businesses can humanize their brand and create a more memorable experience. For instance, a cosmetics company might share stories of real customers who have benefited from their products, highlighting the positive impact on their lives. These stories not only build trust but also make the brand more relatable and authentic.

Building a comprehensive customer profile requires integrating data from multiple sources. This includes transactional data, behavioral data, and attitudinal data. By combining these data points, businesses can create a holistic view of their customers, enabling more personalized and relevant interactions. For example, a travel agency might integrate booking history, website behavior, and customer preferences to recommend tailored travel packages. This level of personalization enhances the customer experience and increases the likelihood of repeat business.

Loyalty programs are an effective way to encourage repeat business and gather valuable data on customer behavior. By offering rewards and incentives for repeat purchases, businesses can foster long-term relationships with their customers. Additionally, loyalty programs provide insights into purchasing patterns and preferences, which can inform marketing and product development strategies. For instance, a coffee shop might use data from its loyalty program to introduce new flavors or seasonal promotions that align with customer preferences.

Incorporating customer behavior insights into product development can lead to more successful products and services. By understanding what customers value and how they use existing products, businesses can identify opportunities for innovation and improvement. For example, a tech company might use customer feedback and usage data to develop new features for its software, addressing pain points and enhancing functionality. Involving customers in the development process through beta testing and feedback loops ensures that the final product meets their needs and expectations.

Customer behavior is not static; it evolves over time. Regularly monitoring and analyzing behavior helps businesses stay ahead of trends and adapt to changing preferences. For example, the rise of mobile shopping has transformed how consumers interact with brands. Businesses that recognize this shift and optimize their mobile presence are better positioned to capture and retain customers. Continuous learning and adaptation are key to maintaining relevance and competitiveness in a dynamic market.

In conclusion, understanding customer behavior is a multifaceted endeavor that requires a combination of data analysis, segmentation, feedback, and external awareness. By gaining a deep understanding of what drives customer decisions, businesses can tailor their strategies to meet the specific needs of their audience. This not only enhances customer satisfaction and loyalty but also drives business growth and success. As customer behavior continues to evolve, businesses must remain agile and responsive, continually seeking new insights and opportunities to better serve their customers. Businesses that invest time and resources in understanding customer behavior often see significant returns. One practical example is personalized marketing. When businesses understand their customers' preferences, habits, and behaviors, they can create highly targeted marketing campaigns that resonate on a personal level. For example, an online retailer might send personalized email recommendations based on a customer's previous purchases and browsing history. This level of personalization increases the likelihood of engagement and conversion, as customers feel that the brand understands and caters to their individual needs.

Case Studies of Market Analysis Successes

Case studies of market analysis successes provide valuable insights into how businesses can effectively leverage market research to achieve their goals. These real-world examples demonstrate the practical application of market analysis techniques and the significant impact they can have on business outcomes. By examining these cases, we can uncover the strategies and decisions that led to success, offering a roadmap for others to follow.

One notable example is the market analysis conducted by Apple prior to the launch of the iPhone. At the time, the mobile phone market was dominated by established players like Nokia and BlackBerry, and the concept of a touchscreen smartphone was still relatively new. Apple undertook extensive market research to understand consumer pain points and preferences. They identified a strong demand for a device that combined a phone, an iPod, and an internet communicator. This insight guided their product development process, leading to the creation of the iPhone, which revolutionized the industry. The success of the iPhone can be attributed to Apple's ability to identify and address unmet needs in the market through thorough analysis.

Another compelling case study is the turnaround story of Domino's Pizza. In the early 2000s, Domino's faced declining sales and a tarnished reputation due to complaints about the quality of their pizza. The company decided to conduct comprehensive market analysis to understand the root causes of customer dissatisfaction. Through surveys, focus groups, and social media monitoring, they gathered candid feedback from customers who criticized the taste and quality of the pizza. Armed with this data, Domino's launched a bold campaign admitting their shortcomings and promising a complete overhaul of their pizza recipe. They invited customers to try the new pizza and share their honest opinions. This transparent approach, combined with a significant improvement in product quality, led to a dramatic increase in sales and a revitalized brand image. Domino's success story highlights the importance of listening to customer feedback and using it to drive meaningful changes.

Netflix's transformation from a DVD rental service to a global streaming giant is another exemplary case of market analysis success. In the mid-2000s, Netflix recognized the growing trend of digital consumption and the decline of physical media. They conducted extensive market research to understand consumer preferences for on-demand content and the limitations of traditional cable television. This analysis revealed a significant opportunity for streaming services that offered convenience and a wide selection of content. Netflix invested heavily in developing a robust streaming platform and acquiring content licenses. They also used data analytics to personalize recommendations and improve the user experience. By anticipating the shift in consumer behavior and capitalizing on it, Netflix was able to dominate the streaming market and become a household name.

A more recent example is the success of Warby Parker, an eyewear company that disrupted the traditional optical industry. Warby Parker's founders identified a gap in the market for affordable, stylish eyewear sold online. They conducted market research to understand consumer frustrations with the high cost of glasses and the inconvenience of traditional retail experiences. This research revealed a strong demand for a direct-to-consumer model that offered both affordability and convenience. Warby Parker launched with a unique home try-on program, allowing customers to try multiple frames at home before making a purchase. They also focused on creating a strong brand identity and an engaging online shopping experience. The company's commitment to understanding and addressing consumer needs propelled them to rapid success, challenging established industry players and setting new standards for customer experience in eyewear retail.

Market analysis also played a crucial role in the successful rebranding of Old Spice. The brand, traditionally associated with older demographics, faced declining sales and relevance among younger consumers. Old Spice conducted market research to understand the preferences and perceptions of their target audience. They discovered that younger consumers responded positively to humor and irreverent advertising. Armed with this insight, Old Spice launched the "Smell Like a Man, Man" campaign featuring humorous and memorable commercials that resonated with the younger demographic. The campaign went viral, revitalizing the brand and significantly increasing sales. Old Spice's ability to adapt their marketing strategy based on market analysis highlights the importance of staying attuned to changing consumer preferences.

In the automotive industry, Tesla's success can be attributed to their market analysis and understanding of consumer trends. Tesla identified a growing interest in sustainable transportation and the limitations of traditional electric vehicles (EVs). Through market research, they understood that consumers desired EVs with longer ranges, better performance, and stylish designs. Tesla focused on addressing these pain points by developing high-performance electric cars with cutting-edge technology and appealing aesthetics. They also invested in creating an extensive charging infrastructure to alleviate range anxiety. By aligning their product development with market demands, Tesla was able to position itself as a leader in the EV market, driving widespread adoption and influencing the entire automotive industry.

Airbnb's rise to prominence is another powerful example of market analysis in action. The founders of Airbnb recognized the potential of the sharing economy and the growing interest in unique, local travel experiences. They conducted market research to understand travelers' preferences and the challenges faced by traditional accommodation providers. This research revealed a strong desire for affordable, authentic, and personalized travel options. Airbnb capitalized on this insight by creating a platform that allowed individuals to rent out their homes or spare rooms to travelers. They also focused on building trust within the community through features like reviews and secure payment systems. Airbnb's success demonstrates how market analysis can uncover untapped opportunities and drive innovation in established industries.

Procter & Gamble's (P&G) success with the Swiffer cleaning products is a testament to the power of market analysis in product development. Before launching Swiffer, P&G conducted extensive research to understand consumers' cleaning habits and pain points. They discovered that people found traditional mops and brooms cumbersome and ineffective for quick cleanups. This insight led to the development of the Swiffer, a convenient and efficient cleaning tool designed to address these issues. P&G's market analysis also revealed a strong demand for disposable cleaning pads, leading to ongoing sales and repeat customers. The Swiffer's success underscores the importance of understanding consumer behavior and pain points to create products that truly meet their needs.

These case studies illustrate the transformative impact of market analysis on business success. By understanding customer needs, preferences, and pain points, companies can develop products and services that resonate with their target audience. Market analysis provides the foundation for informed decision-making, guiding businesses toward strategies that drive growth and innovation. Whether it's through identifying unmet needs, adapting to changing trends, or leveraging consumer feedback, the power of market analysis lies in its ability to turn data into actionable insights. As these examples show, the companies that invest in thorough market analysis are often the ones that achieve remarkable success and set new standards in their industries. These success stories also highlight the importance of agility and responsiveness in market analysis. In a rapidly changing business environment, companies must adapt quickly to new information and emerging trends. A prime example of this is the swift pivot by Zoom Video Communications during the COVID-19 pandemic. Initially catering primarily to corporate clients, Zoom observed a sudden and massive shift in the demand for video conferencing as work-from-home policies were implemented globally. Through real-time market analysis, they identified the need for reliable, user-friendly communication tools for not just businesses, but also schools, social gatherings, and everyday personal use.

Chapter 4

Developing an Innovation Strategy

Setting Innovation Goals

Setting innovation goals is a crucial step for any organization aiming to stay competitive in today's fast-paced market. Innovation is the lifeblood of progress, driving companies to develop new products, enhance services, and improve processes. However, innovation doesn't happen by accident; it requires clear, strategic goals that guide efforts and resources effectively. Crafting these goals involves understanding the company's vision, analyzing market trends, and fostering a culture that encourages creative thinking and calculated risk-taking.

The first step in setting innovation goals is to align them with the overall strategic vision of the organization. This ensures that innovation efforts contribute directly to the company's long-term objectives. For instance, if a tech company's vision is to become the leader in sustainable technology, its innovation goals should focus on developing green technologies or improving energy efficiency in their products. This alignment helps in maintaining a cohesive strategy and utilizing resources effectively.

Understanding market trends and customer needs is another critical component. Companies must conduct thorough market research to identify emerging trends, potential disruptions, and areas where customer needs are not being fully met. This information can provide valuable insights into where innovation is most needed. For example, the rise of remote work has created a demand for better virtual collaboration tools, prompting companies in the tech industry to innovate in this space. By setting innovation goals that address these specific market demands, companies can ensure their efforts are relevant and timely.

Fostering a culture of innovation within the organization is essential for achieving these goals. This involves encouraging employees at all levels to think creatively and take risks. Leaders should create an environment where new ideas are welcomed and failure is seen as a learning opportunity rather than a setback. Google's "20% time" policy, which allows employees to spend 20% of their time on projects that interest them, is a classic example of fostering such a culture. This policy has led to the creation of successful products like Gmail and Google Maps. By setting innovation goals that encourage this kind of environment, companies can tap into the creative potential of their workforce.

Another important aspect of setting innovation goals is defining clear metrics for success. Without measurable objectives, it's difficult to assess progress and make necessary adjustments. These metrics could include the number of new products launched, improvements in customer satisfaction, or reductions in production costs. For example, a goal might be to develop a new product that captures 10% of the market share within two years. Such specific targets provide a clear direction and make it easier to track progress and outcomes.

Collaboration is also vital in the innovation process. Companies should set goals that encourage collaboration both within and outside the organization. Internally, cross-functional teams can bring diverse perspectives and expertise, leading to more robust and creative solutions. Externally, partnerships with other companies, research institutions, and startups can provide access to new technologies and ideas. For instance, the pharmaceutical industry often relies on collaborations with biotech startups to drive innovation in drug development. Setting goals that promote these partnerships can significantly enhance a company's innovation capabilities.

Investing in the right resources is another key factor. Innovation requires time, funding, and talent. Companies must be willing to allocate sufficient resources to their innovation initiatives. This might involve setting up dedicated innovation labs, investing in research and development, or hiring experts in emerging technologies. For example, Tesla's significant investment in battery technology has been a crucial factor in its success in the electric vehicle market. By setting goals that prioritize resource allocation for innovation, companies can ensure they have the necessary tools to achieve their ambitions.

It's also important to balance short-term and long-term innovation goals. While it's essential to deliver quick wins to maintain momentum and demonstrate progress, companies should also invest in long-term projects that might take years to bear fruit. This balance ensures sustainable innovation and avoids the pitfall of focusing only on immediate gains. For instance, while developing incremental improvements to existing products, companies should also invest in breakthrough technologies that can disrupt the market in the future.

Leadership plays a crucial role in setting and achieving innovation goals. Leaders must champion the cause of innovation, providing a clear vision and motivating their teams to pursue ambitious goals. They should communicate the importance of innovation in achieving the company's objectives and recognize and reward innovative efforts. Leadership's commitment to innovation can inspire the entire organization to embrace a culture of continuous improvement and creativity.

Regular review and adjustment of innovation goals are also necessary. The business environment and market conditions are constantly evolving, and companies must be agile in their approach. Regularly reviewing innovation goals allows companies to assess their progress, learn from their experiences, and make necessary adjustments to stay on track. This iterative process ensures that innovation efforts remain relevant and aligned with the company's strategic direction.

Finally, celebrating successes and learning from failures are important practices in the innovation journey. Recognizing and celebrating achievements boosts morale and reinforces the importance of innovation. Equally, analyzing failures and understanding what went wrong provide valuable lessons that can inform future efforts. This balanced approach helps in building a resilient and innovative organization.

In conclusion, setting innovation goals is a strategic process that involves aligning with the company's vision, understanding market trends, fostering a culture of innovation, defining clear metrics, encouraging collaboration, investing in the right resources, balancing short-term and long-term goals, demonstrating leadership commitment, regularly reviewing progress, and learning from both successes and failures. By following these principles, companies can create a robust framework for innovation that drives growth and maintains competitive advantage in an ever-changing market landscape. To truly embed these principles into the fabric of the organization, it's crucial to integrate innovation goals into the performance management system. This means that innovation should be a key performance indicator (KPI) for teams and individuals across the company. By doing so, employees are directly accountable for contributing to the company's innovation agenda, ensuring that these goals are not just aspirational but actionable and measured.

Aligning Innovation with Business Strategy

Aligning innovation with business strategy is essential for companies aiming to achieve sustainable growth and maintain a competitive edge. This alignment ensures that all innovative efforts contribute to the overarching goals of the organization, thus maximizing their impact. It requires a clear understanding of the company's vision, its strategic objectives, and the dynamic market environment in which it operates. By harmonizing innovation with business strategy, companies can effectively channel their resources and creativity towards initiatives that drive meaningful progress.

Understanding the company's vision is the first critical step. The vision statement outlines the long-term aspirations of the company and serves as a guiding star for all strategic decisions. It reflects what the company aims to become and the value it seeks to provide to its customers and stakeholders. For instance, a firm with a vision to be a leader in sustainable technology will prioritize innovations that reduce environmental impact. The innovation goals must, therefore, be crafted to support this vision, ensuring that new products, services, or processes align with the broader mission of the company.

Once the vision is clear, it is crucial to break it down into strategic objectives. These objectives are more specific and actionable, providing a roadmap for achieving the vision. They might include targets such as entering new markets, increasing market share, improving customer satisfaction, or driving operational efficiencies. Each of these objectives offers a focal point for innovation efforts. For example, if one of the strategic objectives is to enter new markets, innovation might focus on developing products that cater to the unique needs of those markets or finding new distribution channels.

Market analysis plays a pivotal role in aligning innovation with business strategy. Companies must keep a pulse on market trends, customer preferences, and competitive dynamics. This involves continuous market research to identify opportunities and threats.

For example, the growing demand for electric vehicles presents a significant opportunity for automotive companies. By understanding this trend, a company can align its innovation efforts towards developing electric vehicles and related technologies. This not only meets market demand but also positions the company strategically against its competitors.

A robust innovation strategy is built on the foundation of this market intelligence. It involves setting clear innovation goals that support the strategic objectives and are informed by market insights. For example, if a company's strategic objective is to enhance customer satisfaction, its innovation goals might include developing new features or services that address customer pain points. These goals should be specific, measurable, achievable, relevant, and time-bound (SMART) to ensure they drive tangible outcomes.

Leadership commitment is crucial in this alignment process. Leaders must communicate the importance of innovation in achieving the company's strategic goals and create an environment that fosters creative thinking and experimentation. They should also allocate resources—time, funding, and talent— towards innovation initiatives that align with the business strategy. For instance, establishing dedicated innovation teams or labs can provide the necessary infrastructure to support these efforts. Leadership should also be involved in regularly reviewing and adjusting innovation goals to ensure they remain aligned with the evolving business strategy.

Cross-functional collaboration within the organization can significantly enhance the alignment of innovation and business strategy. When departments such as

R&D, marketing, sales, and operations work together, they can combine their diverse perspectives and expertise to drive innovation that supports strategic objectives. For example, the marketing team's insights into customer needs can inform the R&D team's development of new products. Similarly, the operations team can provide valuable input on how to streamline production processes, ensuring that innovations are not only market-relevant but also operationally feasible.

Establishing clear metrics for innovation performance is another essential aspect. These metrics should be directly linked to the strategic objectives and provide a basis for evaluating the success of innovation initiatives. For example, if a strategic objective is to increase market share, relevant innovation metrics might include the number of new products launched, their market penetration, and revenue growth from new products. Regularly tracking these metrics helps in assessing progress and making necessary adjustments to keep innovation efforts aligned with business strategy.

Fostering a culture that supports innovation is equally important. This involves encouraging a mindset that values creativity, experimentation, and learning from failure. Companies can achieve this by recognizing and rewarding innovative efforts, providing training and development opportunities, and promoting open communication and idea sharing. For example, a company might implement an internal innovation contest where employees can pitch their ideas, with the best ones receiving funding and support for development. Such initiatives not only generate new ideas but also reinforce the importance of innovation in achieving strategic goals.

Investing in the right technologies and tools can also facilitate the alignment of innovation with business strategy. Digital tools for data analysis, project management, and collaboration can streamline innovation processes and enhance decision-making. For instance, data analytics can provide insights into customer behavior and preferences, informing innovation efforts. Project management tools can help in tracking the progress of innovation projects and ensuring they stay on course. Collaboration platforms can enable seamless communication and idea sharing across different teams and geographies.

External partnerships and collaborations can further strengthen this alignment. Companies can benefit from collaborating with startups, universities, research institutions, and other organizations that bring in new perspectives and expertise. For example, partnering with a tech startup can provide access to cutting-edge technologies that can drive innovation. Similarly, collaborating with academic institutions can facilitate research and development of new solutions. By setting innovation goals that include external partnerships, companies can leverage external resources and insights to support their strategic objectives.

Regular review and iteration of innovation goals are necessary to ensure they remain aligned with the business strategy. The business environment is dynamic, and strategic priorities may shift in response to new opportunities or challenges. Companies should establish a process for regularly reviewing their innovation goals and adjusting them as needed. This might involve quarterly or annual reviews where leadership assesses the progress of innovation initiatives and makes necessary adjustments to align with any changes in the strategic direction.

Celebrating successes and learning from failures are important practices in this journey. Recognizing and celebrating successful innovation projects not only boosts morale but also reinforces the strategic importance of innovation. On the other hand, analyzing and learning from failures provide valuable lessons that can inform future efforts. Companies should create an environment where failure is seen as a learning opportunity, encouraging teams to take calculated risks and experiment with new ideas.

In conclusion, aligning innovation with business strategy is a multifaceted process that involves understanding the company's vision, setting strategic objectives, conducting market analysis, fostering a supportive culture, ensuring leadership commitment, facilitating cross-functional collaboration, establishing clear metrics, leveraging technology, engaging in external partnerships, and regularly reviewing and iterating goals. By following these principles, companies can ensure that their innovation efforts are not only well-directed but also capable of driving significant growth and maintaining a competitive edge in an ever-evolving market landscape. This harmonious alignment is key to unlocking the full potential of innovation and achieving long-term success. To deepen the implementation of these principles, it's essential to embed innovation into the fundamental processes of the organization. One effective approach is to incorporate innovation into the strategic planning process. This means that during annual or quarterly strategic planning sessions, innovation should be a core agenda item. By doing so, companies can ensure that innovation is not treated as a separate or secondary activity but as an integral part of the business strategy.

Risk Management in Innovation

Risk management in innovation is a critical aspect of ensuring that new initiatives not only succeed but also contribute positively to the overall strategic goals of an organization. Innovation inherently comes with a degree of uncertainty, and managing this uncertainty effectively can be the difference between groundbreaking success and costly failure. By understanding and mitigating risks, companies can create an environment where innovation thrives while still maintaining control over potential downsides.

Every innovation initiative begins with an idea, but before diving headfirst into development, it's essential to conduct a thorough risk assessment. This assessment involves identifying potential risks that could derail the project. These risks can be categorized into various types: market risks, financial risks, technical risks, and operational risks. Market risks involve uncertainties about customer acceptance and market demand. Financial risks pertain to budget overruns and funding shortages. Technical risks relate to the feasibility of developing the innovation and integrating it into existing systems. Operational risks encompass the day-to-day challenges of implementing and scaling the innovation.

To illustrate, consider a company developing a new wearable fitness device. Market risks might include whether there is enough demand for another fitness tracker in an already saturated market. Financial risks could involve the initial capital required for research and development, as well as the marketing budget needed to promote the product. Technical risks might include the challenges of creating a device that accurately tracks various fitness metrics and syncs seamlessly with users' smartphones. Operational risks could involve the logistics of manufacturing and distributing the device on a large scale.

Once risks are identified, the next step is to evaluate their potential impact and likelihood. This can be done using a risk matrix, which plots the probability of each risk occurring against its potential impact on the project. Risks that fall into the high-impact, high-likelihood quadrant require immediate and robust mitigation strategies. For example, if there is a high risk that the market may not respond favorably to the new fitness device, the company might conduct extensive market research or launch a pilot program to gauge interest before full-scale production.

Effective risk management also involves developing contingency plans for the highest-priority risks. These plans outline specific actions that will be taken if a risk materializes. For instance, if technical challenges arise in developing the fitness tracker, the company might have a contingency plan to collaborate with technology experts or outsource certain aspects of development to specialized firms. Having these plans in place ensures that the project can continue moving forward even when unexpected issues arise.

Another important aspect of risk management in innovation is fostering a culture of transparency and open communication. Teams should feel comfortable discussing potential risks and challenges without fear of retribution. This openness allows for early identification of issues and collective problem-solving. For example, regular project meetings where team members discuss progress and potential obstacles can help keep everyone informed and engaged in managing risks proactively.

Involving stakeholders early and often in the innovation process can also mitigate risks. Stakeholders, including customers, partners, and investors, can provide valuable insights and feedback that help identify potential pitfalls. For instance, engaging with potential users of the fitness device during the development phase can reveal design flaws or feature gaps that might not have been apparent internally. This collaborative approach not only reduces the risk of market rejection but also builds a sense of ownership and support among stakeholders.

Risk management should also be integrated into the company's overall innovation strategy. This means that risk considerations should be part of the criteria for selecting and prioritizing innovation projects. Projects with unmanageable risks or those that do not align with the company's risk tolerance should be reconsidered or restructured. For example, if the company's strategic goal is to enhance its reputation for reliability, pursuing a high-risk project that could result in significant operational disruptions might be counterproductive.

Additionally, companies should invest in building their risk management capabilities. This includes training employees on risk assessment and mitigation techniques, as well as developing tools and frameworks for systematic risk management. For example, workshops on risk management can equip innovation teams with the skills needed to identify and address risks effectively. Developing a standardized risk management framework ensures consistency and thoroughness across different projects.

Monitoring and reviewing risks throughout the innovation lifecycle is crucial. Risks are not static; they can evolve as the project progresses and new information becomes available. Regular risk reviews allow teams to reassess the risk landscape and adjust their mitigation strategies accordingly. For example, if new competitors enter the market while the fitness device is still in development, the company might need to accelerate its timeline or enhance its product features to maintain a competitive edge.

Learning from past projects is another vital component of effective risk management. Conducting post-mortem analyses on completed projects, whether they succeeded or failed, can provide valuable lessons that inform future initiatives. Understanding what went wrong and what worked well helps in refining risk management practices. For instance, if a previous innovation project failed due to underestimating technical challenges, future projects can benefit from more rigorous technical feasibility assessments.

Implementing risk management in innovation also involves balancing risk and reward. Not all risks should be avoided; some are worth taking for the potential benefits they offer. The key is to make informed decisions based on a clear understanding of the risks and their potential impact. For example, a company might decide to pursue a high-risk, high-reward project if it aligns with its strategic goals and there are adequate mitigation strategies in place.

Finally, it's important to recognize that risk management in innovation is an ongoing process. It requires continuous attention and adaptation as the project evolves and new risks emerge. By embedding risk management into the fabric of the innovation process, companies can create a resilient and agile approach to developing new products, services, and solutions. This proactive stance not only enhances the likelihood of success but also builds a culture of preparedness and resilience that can navigate the uncertainties of the innovation landscape.

In conclusion, managing risk in innovation involves a comprehensive approach that includes identifying, evaluating, and mitigating potential risks, fostering a culture of transparency and collaboration, integrating risk considerations into strategic decision-making, building risk management capabilities, and continuously monitoring and learning from past projects. By adopting these practices, companies can navigate the uncertainties of innovation, turn potential pitfalls into opportunities, and achieve sustainable growth and success in an ever-evolving market. One of the most powerful tools for managing risk in innovation is scenario planning. This involves envisioning multiple future scenarios and developing strategies to address each one. Scenario planning helps organizations prepare for a range of possible outcomes, making them more resilient to unexpected changes. For example, in developing the wearable fitness device, scenario planning might include envisioning scenarios where the device becomes a market leader, where it faces stiff competition, or where it struggles to gain traction. For each scenario, the company would develop a set of strategies to either capitalize on opportunities or mitigate challenges.

Creating a Roadmap for Innovation

Creating a roadmap for innovation is essential for any organization looking to bring new ideas from concept to reality. This strategic plan serves as a guide, detailing the steps and resources needed to achieve innovation goals. A well-crafted roadmap aligns the innovation efforts with the company's vision, ensuring that every stakeholder understands their role in the journey. It also helps in anticipating challenges and allocating resources efficiently, thus increasing the likelihood of success.

The first step in creating an innovation roadmap is to define the vision and objectives. This involves understanding what the organization aims to achieve through its innovation efforts. The vision should be ambitious yet attainable, inspiring the team while providing clear direction. For example, a technology company might set a vision to become the market leader in sustainable energy solutions within five years. This vision then translates into specific objectives, such as developing new products, entering new markets, or enhancing existing technologies.

Once the vision and objectives are set, the next step is to conduct a thorough assessment of the current state of the organization. This includes evaluating existing resources, capabilities, and market position. Understanding the starting point is crucial for planning the journey ahead. For instance, if the company already has a strong research and development team but lacks marketing expertise, the roadmap might prioritize building marketing capabilities or partnering with marketing firms.

Identifying key stakeholders and involving them early in the process is also critical. Stakeholders can include employees, customers, investors, and partners. Their input and buy-in are essential for the success of the innovation roadmap. Engaging stakeholders can be achieved through workshops, surveys, and regular communication. For example, involving customers in the early stages of product development can provide valuable insights into their needs and preferences, ensuring that the innovation efforts are aligned with market demands.

With a clear understanding of the vision, objectives, and current state, the next step is to identify and prioritize innovation initiatives. These initiatives can range from incremental improvements to breakthrough innovations. Prioritization should be based on factors such as strategic alignment, potential impact, feasibility, and resource requirements. For example, a company might prioritize initiatives that have a high potential for market differentiation and align closely with its core competencies.

Developing a detailed action plan for each initiative is the next crucial step. This plan should outline the specific tasks, timelines, milestones, and responsible parties. Breaking down the initiatives into manageable tasks helps in tracking progress and maintaining momentum. For instance, if the initiative is to develop a new product, the action plan might include tasks such as market research, prototype development, testing, and launching. Each task should have a clear timeline and assigned team members to ensure accountability.

Resource allocation is another important aspect of creating an innovation roadmap. This includes not only financial resources but also human resources, technology, and infrastructure. Effective resource allocation ensures that each initiative has the necessary support to succeed. For example, a company might allocate a dedicated budget for research and development, hire additional staff with specialized skills, or invest in new technologies that facilitate innovation. It's also important to build flexibility into the resource allocation process, allowing for adjustments as the project evolves.

Risk management should be integrated into the roadmap from the beginning. Innovation inherently involves uncertainty, and identifying potential risks early allows for proactive mitigation strategies. This might involve conducting risk assessments for each initiative, developing contingency plans, and continuously monitoring for new risks. For example, if an initiative depends heavily on a new technology, the roadmap should include plans for alternative solutions in case the technology fails to meet expectations.

Communication and transparency are vital throughout the innovation process. Keeping all stakeholders informed about progress, challenges, and changes helps maintain alignment and support. Regular updates can be provided through meetings, reports, or digital platforms. For example, a monthly newsletter might highlight key milestones achieved, upcoming tasks, and any changes to the roadmap. Transparent communication fosters a culture of trust and collaboration, which is essential for driving innovation.

Tracking progress and measuring success are critical components of an effective innovation roadmap. This involves setting key performance indicators (KPIs) that align with the objectives and regularly reviewing them to assess progress. KPIs might include metrics such as time-to-market, cost savings, revenue from new products, or customer satisfaction. Regular reviews help identify any deviations from the plan and allow for course corrections. For example, if a new product launch is delayed, the team can analyze the cause and adjust the timeline or resources accordingly.

Flexibility and adaptability are also key to a successful innovation roadmap. The business environment is constantly changing, and the roadmap should be able to evolve in response to new information, market shifts, or emerging opportunities. This might involve revisiting the vision and objectives periodically, reassessing priorities, and making necessary adjustments. For example, if a competitor launches a similar product, the company might need to accelerate its own development timeline or enhance its features to maintain a competitive edge.

Celebrating milestones and successes along the way is important for maintaining motivation and momentum. Recognizing the efforts and achievements of the team fosters a positive and innovative culture. This can be done through awards, public recognition, or team celebrations. For example, celebrating the successful launch of a new product with a company-wide event not only acknowledges the hard work of the team but also reinforces the value of innovation within the organization.

Creating a roadmap for innovation is not a one-time task but an ongoing process. It requires continuous monitoring, feedback, and adjustments to stay on track and achieve the desired outcomes. Regularly reviewing the roadmap and incorporating lessons learned from each initiative helps in refining the approach and improving future innovation efforts. For example, conducting post-implementation reviews for each initiative can provide valuable insights into what worked well and what could be improved, informing future projects.

The role of leadership in driving the innovation roadmap cannot be overstated. Leaders set the vision, provide direction, and inspire the team to pursue ambitious goals. They also play a crucial role in fostering a culture of innovation and ensuring that the necessary resources and support are in place. Effective leaders communicate the importance of the innovation roadmap, align it with the overall business strategy, and empower their teams to take ownership of their initiatives. For example, a CEO who regularly communicates the strategic importance of innovation and recognizes the contributions of the innovation team can significantly enhance the organization's innovation capabilities.

In summary, creating a roadmap for innovation involves a comprehensive and strategic approach that includes defining the vision and objectives, assessing the current state, engaging stakeholders, prioritizing initiatives, developing action plans, allocating resources, managing risks, ensuring communication and transparency, tracking progress, and maintaining flexibility. By following these steps and continuously refining the approach, organizations can navigate the complexities of innovation, successfully bring new ideas to market, and achieve sustainable growth and competitive advantage. An effective innovation roadmap is dynamic and evolves with the organization. It's important to embed a culture of continuous improvement and learning within the team. This means not only celebrating successes but also embracing failures as opportunities for growth. When a project doesn't go as planned, it's crucial to conduct a thorough analysis to understand what went wrong and how similar issues can be avoided in the future. This iterative learning process strengthens the organization's innovation capabilities over time.

Measuring Innovation Success

Measuring innovation success is critical for understanding the impact of your efforts and steering future initiatives. It involves evaluating both the tangible and intangible outcomes of innovation activities, ensuring that they align with the strategic goals of the organization. This process is not only about assessing the financial returns but also about understanding how innovation contributes to overall growth, market positioning, and long-term sustainability.

One of the primary ways to measure innovation success is through financial metrics. These include revenue growth, profit margins, and return on investment (ROI). For instance, introducing a new product that significantly boosts sales can be a clear indicator of successful innovation. However, relying solely on financial metrics can be limiting, as they often reflect only the short-term impact. Long-term measures, such as the lifetime value of customers gained through innovative products or services, provide a more comprehensive view. For example, a company that introduces a subscription-based service might initially see modest revenue increases, but the long-term customer loyalty and recurring revenue streams can be substantial indicators of success.

Market performance metrics are also essential. These include market share, customer acquisition rates, and penetration into new markets. For instance, if an organization launches an innovative product that captures a significant portion of the market, this is a strong sign of success. Additionally, the ability to enter and establish a presence in new markets reflects the effectiveness of your innovation strategy. For example, a tech company launching its products in an emerging market and quickly gaining a foothold suggests that its innovation efforts are resonating with new customer segments.

Customer-centric metrics provide valuable insights into the success of innovation. These include customer satisfaction, Net Promoter Score (NPS), and customer retention rates. High customer satisfaction and NPS indicate that the innovation is meeting or exceeding customer expectations. For instance, if a new app receives consistently high ratings and positive reviews, it's a clear signal that the innovation is successful. Retention rates are equally important; if customers continue to use and renew your product or service, it shows that your innovation has lasting value.

Operational efficiency metrics are crucial for assessing how innovation improves internal processes. These can include productivity gains, cost savings, and reductions in time-to-market. For example, if a manufacturing company adopts a new technology that significantly reduces production time and costs, this operational efficiency translates into successful innovation. Similarly, if a software development team implements a new agile methodology that speeds up product releases without compromising quality, it's a clear indicator of innovation success.

Employee-related metrics should not be overlooked. Innovation often requires a motivated and engaged workforce. Metrics such as employee engagement, retention, and the number of new ideas generated can provide insights into the internal impact of innovation efforts. For instance, a company that fosters a culture of innovation might see an increase in employee satisfaction and a higher retention rate, indicating that employees feel valued and excited about contributing to innovative projects.

It's also important to consider the strategic alignment of innovation initiatives. Success can be measured by how well these initiatives align with the organization's long-term goals and vision. For example, if a company has a strategic objective to become a leader in sustainable technology, the success of its innovation efforts can be measured by the development and market adoption of eco-friendly products. This alignment ensures that innovation is not just about short-term gains but also about building a sustainable competitive advantage.

Qualitative measures, while sometimes harder to quantify, are equally important. These can include customer feedback, industry recognition, and brand perception. Positive customer testimonials and case studies can provide compelling evidence of innovation success. Industry awards and recognition validate the organization's efforts and enhance its reputation. For instance, receiving an industry award for a groundbreaking product not only boosts morale but also strengthens the company's market position.

Benchmarking against competitors is another valuable approach. By comparing your innovation performance with that of your competitors, you can gain insights into your relative strengths and weaknesses. This can involve analyzing competitor products, market strategies, and customer feedback. For example, if your competitors are consistently launching more successful products, it may indicate a need to refine your innovation processes. Conversely, if you're outperforming competitors, it validates your innovation strategy.

Tracking the innovation pipeline is crucial for ongoing success. This involves monitoring the progress of various innovation projects from idea generation to market launch. Metrics such as the number of ideas in the pipeline, the conversion rate of ideas to projects, and the time taken to move from concept to commercialization provide a clear picture of the efficiency and effectiveness of your innovation process. For example, a high conversion rate indicates a robust process for vetting and developing viable ideas.

Innovation ecosystems and partnerships also play a role in measuring success. Collaborations with external partners, such as startups, research institutions, and other organizations, can enhance innovation capabilities. Metrics such as the number of successful partnerships, joint ventures, and co-developed products can provide insights into the effectiveness of your innovation ecosystem. For instance, a successful collaboration that leads to a new market-ready product demonstrates the value of external partnerships in driving innovation.

Employee innovation engagement is another key metric. Encouraging employees to contribute ideas and participate in innovation initiatives can lead to valuable insights and solutions. Tracking the number of ideas submitted, the diversity of participants, and the implementation rate of employee-generated ideas can provide a clear indication of how engaged and innovative your workforce is. For example, a company that regularly implements employee suggestions and sees tangible improvements in products or processes is effectively leveraging its internal talent for innovation.

Environmental and social impact metrics are increasingly important, especially for organizations with a focus on sustainability and corporate social responsibility. These metrics can include the reduction of carbon footprint, improvements in energy efficiency, and contributions to social causes. For instance, if a company's innovation efforts lead to a significant reduction in energy consumption across its operations, it demonstrates a successful alignment with sustainability goals. Similarly, innovations that improve community well-being or address social issues reflect positively on the organization's broader impact.

Regularly reviewing and refining the metrics used to measure innovation success is essential. As the business environment evolves, so too should the criteria for success. This might involve introducing new metrics, discontinuing outdated ones, or adjusting the weight given to various measures. For example, as digital transformation becomes more critical, metrics related to digital adoption and performance may gain prominence in assessing innovation success.

In summary, measuring innovation success requires a multifaceted approach that encompasses financial performance, market impact, customer satisfaction, operational efficiency, employee engagement, strategic alignment, qualitative feedback, competitive benchmarking, innovation pipeline tracking, partnership effectiveness, and environmental and social impact. By adopting a comprehensive and dynamic set of metrics, organizations can gain a holistic understanding of their innovation efforts, make informed decisions, and continuously improve their innovation processes. This approach not only ensures that innovation initiatives deliver tangible results but also fosters a culture of continuous improvement, driving long-term success and sustainability. Ultimately, the goal of measuring innovation success is to create a feedback loop that informs and enhances future innovation efforts. This involves not only gathering data but also analyzing it to extract actionable insights. For instance, if customer feedback indicates that a new product feature is particularly well-received, this insight can guide the development of similar features in future products. Conversely, if certain innovations fail to meet expectations, understanding the root causes can help avoid similar pitfalls.